Carolyn Pogue

PART-TIME
PARENT

Learning to Live
without
Full-Time Custody

Northstone

Editor: Michael Schwartzentruber
Cover design: Margaret Kyle
Interior design: Julie Bachewich
Consulting art director: Robert MacDonald

Part-Time Parent was originally published by Western Producer Prairie Books,
Saskatoon, Saskatchewan, 1990, as *The Weekend Parent:
Learning to Live without Full-time Kids*.

Northstone Publishing acknowledges the financial support of the Government of Canada
through the Book Publishing Industry Development Program for its publishing activities.

Northstone Publishing is an imprint of Wood Lake Books Inc., an employee-owned
company, and is committed to caring for the environment and all creation.
Northstone recycles, reuses, and composts, and encourages readers to do the same.
Resources are printed on recycled paper and more environmentally friendly
groundwood papers (newsprint), whenever possible. The trees used are replaced
through donations to the Scoutrees for Canada program.
Ten percent of all profit is donated to charitable organizations.

Canadian Cataloguing in Publication Data
Pogue, Carolyn, 1948-
Part-time Parent

Includes bibliographical references.
Previous ed. has title: The weekend parent.
ISBN 1-896836-23-2

1. Parenting, Part-time. 2. Divorced parents. 3. Children of divorced parents.
I. Title. II. Title: The weekend parent
HQ755.8.P65 1998   306.85'6   C98-910633-0

Published by Northstone Publishing, an imprint of Wood Lake Books Publishing Inc.
Kelowna, BC

Printing 10 9 8 7 6 5 4 3 2 1

Printed in Canada by Transcontinental Printing & Graphics Inc.

Dedication

To all parents and all children
who must learn to live together
part-time.

Contents

Acknowledgments

Thank you to the women and men who shared their stories with me. This is their book, too.

Thank you to my parents, Ruth and Clayton Pogue, who supported me morally and financially throughout the writing of this book.

Thank you Alberta Culture, Film and Literary Arts, for financial assistance for the original edition of this book.

Thank you to Erica, Gwen and Laverne for encouragement and helpful comments about the manuscript.

Thank you, finally, to Bill, who believes in me.

Edmonton 1989

In the ten years since I first wrote this book, much has changed. What has not changed is that parents continue to live apart from their children because of separation and divorce. To the parents and professionals who have written to me over the years with their reactions to the book and to tell me their own stories, I say thank you for encouragement and for sharing part of your lives. To Michael Schwartzentruber, my editor at Northstone, I say thank you for working with me to bring this book to new life. To Bill and to Andrea, who continue to believe in me, *l'chaim!*

Calgary 1998

Preface

This is not a book about men's rights, women's rights, children's rights. This is not a book of statistics, but of real people. It is not a scientific or sociological study. It is a compilation of stories of 20 men and women I interviewed in five provinces, all of whom had lost custody of their children through separation or divorce.

I asked basic questions: How did it happen? What was it like at first? What is it like now? How did you handle the first traditional celebrations? What would you say to someone who lost custody today? Do you feel guilty? Who are you now? Where is the hope? For the most part, people just talked. I have arranged the material according to these questions and the themes that emerged.

The main purpose of the book is simple: to help noncustodial parents know they are not alone and to provide them with the experiences and practical advice of others in the same situation.

I hope that others will find this book useful, too – counselors, clergy, and friends and families of noncustodial parents. Older children may find some insight here as to why their parent behaved the way he or she did.

The interviews were usually conducted in people's homes, using a tape recorder. All of the people seemed relieved to talk about their feelings. My fear was of running out of tape, not words.

I have not attempted to show both sides of the custody issue, and I make no apology for that. These are the stories of parents without kids. These are our feelings and our perceptions of events. The "other side" is for other books.

This book is for the men and women who opened a deep wound and let the tears and bewilderment and fear and anger come out. They trusted me with their stories and I thank them for that.

All names, locations, and personal details have been changed.

1

Point of Departure

*In all the unhappy daydreams I had about living as a
divorced person, never in a million years did I dream I'd be
without my children. Never once.*

In all the unhappy daydreams I had about living as a divorced person, never in a million years did I dream I'd be without my children. Never once.

Thirteen months after the initial separation, the yo-yo string snapped: I became a childless parent. I was terrified. I wasn't terrified of being alone; I was terrified that my children would think I didn't love them.

In this book you will read stories about what happens when parents lose custody of their children. This loss is different from the loss when a child dies. It is different from the loss when a child grows up and marries or goes away to school or a job in another town.

There are thousands of parents without kids across the country, even though the trend toward joint custody has begun and studies show that children who have open access to both parents seem to do better.[1]

There are tricks to joint custody, however. Parents who can do it successfully are able to separate their married lives from their lives as parents and generally have co-parented inside the marriage. Furthermore, parents must agree to live near one another for the duration of their child-rearing years.

So many divorces are bitter; all of them are sad. Sometimes children are thought of as the "prize" for the "winner." The "loser" goes home alone.

Adults who have open access to their children do better, too. Even though the grief of divorce was horrendous, for me, the grief of losing my children has been much more difficult.

In Bruce Fisher's hope-filled book *Rebuilding: When Your Relationship Ends*, Virginia M. Satir writes, "The emotional levels one needs to work through during and following divorce are very much parallel to the stages one goes through at the time of death."[2] She lists denial, anger, shock, bargaining, depression (including self-hatred, self-blame, and feelings of failure), and, finally, acceptance of the situation and of the self.

I believe her. I also believe that noncustodial parents must work through their grief for the loss of each child, because although the bond may still be there, the parent-child relationship has changed irrevocably.

When I faced squarely the fact that I would no longer be a full-time mother, I went to a counselor. The situation was just too big for me to handle alone. I perused the contents of her bookshelves searching for wise words of comfort and suggestions to help me. The books, alas, assumed that I was the one with the children. They explained how to find a good daycare center and offered me recipes for cheap cuts of meat. I took the recipes but threw out the rest of the information.

While I don't doubt that single parenthood is lonely, exhausting, frustrating, and at times frightening, there has been a great deal written about it. Even television situation comedies feature single parents and their struggles.

Noncustodial parents face the demons within and, unfortunately, they face the demons without, too. Demons that arise from the words of well-meaning friends. "How can you live without your children? I couldn't," is a common comment.

In *Mothers on Trial*, Phyllis Chesler writes,

Mothers who grew too *obsessed* with their lawsuits were often shunned by relatives and friends. Mothers were warned that they would "go mad," "kill themselves," or lose their ability to remarry if they didn't adopt a more positive view of things.

However, a noncustodial mother who tried to "get on" with her life was also perceived as "cold," "unnatural," and "unfit" – *as a person*. Noncustodial mothers became "invisible pariahs," who were condemned or ostracized by other mothers for their noncustodial status.[3]

I believe that noncustodial fathers face equally bizarre, but different, demons. The expectation for men is that they will "get on with it." For women it is that they will wear a hair shirt forever. Both are invisible victims in the matter of divorce and custody, the game in which no one really wins. A parent without kids has lost more than an emotional, legal, and /or financial battle; he or she has lost a center.

Jacqueline Kennedy Onassis says in Bill Adler's book *Motherhood: A Celebration*, "If you bungle raising your children, I don't think whatever else you do matters very much."[4] She puts into words what so many feel and fear.

In many ways, children are worshipped in our society. The onus is on parents to know everything at once, from providing nutrition and managing toilet training to dealing with drugs and alcohol. All of us try, and most of us experience failure at one time or another. There's always a new book that says the last one you read about teaching Myrtle to count, for instance, has not only failed to help your child, but may have even caused damage. In spite of parenting advice in books and magazines, along with our commitment to special programs and child counselors in our schools, none of us is perfectly sure that what we're doing is the best for each individual child.

When I was married, I had only two friends who were willing to admit that parenting (even of preteens) is tough. All the rest lied. I was never sure I was doing it right. Although my parents, my children, my friends, and even my husband had told me I was a good mother, I always thought I should be doing it better. When Judgment Day came, it seemed to confirm my worst fears.

Enter: The Divorce. Custody.

I remember getting the phone call from my lawyer. "You'd better sit down," he said. His reassurance that "custody orders are never carved in stone" did nothing to alter the picture I had in my mind of a black-robed judge pounding his gavel against me. The picture changed from a judge's face to God's. I'd been right all along. I should have done it differently. Even the good judge thinks so.

It's unnatural for parents who have paced the floor with their teething infant to not pace the floor on their teenager's first date. It's not knowing that's so hard. A poorly photocopied report card arriving weeks late in the mail is an ugly thing. Reading it is silent and lonely.

In *Mothers on Trial*, a woman writes, "A force larger than myself visited me during labor. That sense of being at one with God never left me. It sustained me during a violent marriage. It gave me the courage to leave. Unfortunately, it didn't prepare me to live without knowing whether my son is dead or alive."[5]

No book can help people prepare for not knowing if a child is alive or dead. But perhaps this book can help others who are struggling through this dark time when the whole world caves in. We can gather strength from each other. Although we may not understand all the intricacies of the hows and whys and wherefores, we can show that we care for each other.

This book is full of stories of how men and women live through this painful period. There are practical suggestions, self-help, kid-help, and a little homegrown philosophy about our strange new parental status.

In the end, no one gains from bitterness. When we *do* see our children, we want to show them our joy at their being alive, not despair about a situation they neither created nor can alter. We want to show them love and give them our best.

Whether we see them next week or next month or sometime next year, we want to show them the face of someone who loves them. For any parent, that's the most important thing in the world.

2

Like a Play Gone Wrong

"So now you're my ex-mother," she said.
We were riding a bus at the time.
I guess the driver really floored it
because suddenly the whole world looked blurry.

Once upon a time, we all had our parts to play: mother, father, oldest child, youngest child, and so on. Then one day we wrote down our roles on little pieces of paper, put them in a jar, and shook it. We didn't notice that the jar had water in it. We pulled out a new paper and the writing was all washed away. Everyone got mixed up; no one knew who to be.

Children assumed adult responsibilities. Adults acted like children. Adults who had worked, stopped. Adults who hadn't worked, started. Adults who had never cooked put on aprons. Adults who'd always cooked took them off.

It was a crazy play. All the actors improvised desperately. And where was the director? The scriptwriter? No one knew.

That's a little of what the end of my marriage and the subsequent loss of custody felt like to me. Even my mother, thousands of kilometers away, felt it. On the phone she said, "No one in the family has ever done this before, Carolyn. I don't know what to say. What are my lines?"

Most of us reach the end of our marriages in a state of grief, anger, or exhaustion. We have run the race and lost. We have called on all our inner resources. We are tired. Maybe if some of us knew that more anger, grief, self-doubt, and pain lay around the corner, we'd turn back; but I don't think so.

Noncustodial parents find their roles changed overnight. One day they are with the children, the next day they are not. "Getting there" is a little different for each of us, but many of the feelings we have are the same. We carry on, robotlike, until we are able to play our new roles, whatever they may be, with a little confidence.

In spite of what some say, I believe that people *do* take marriage seriously. Divorce, especially when children are involved, is not the easy way out. No one would choose this path unless he or she felt forced to. In a hopelessly unhappy marriage, divorce seems the only logical way out.

These tired, sad people must decide how to care for their children. Ideally, they would sit down together, shelve their marriage problems, and deal with those of parenting. If they could not do this alone, a trained professional called a mediator could help the family or couple decide how to separate with as much dignity and fairness as possible. Mediation is the trend. Unfortunately, most couples still don't do it; those who try aren't always successful.

Our laws have made divorce less complicated for everyone. For example, under the Canadian Divorce Act, 1986, there is only one ground for divorce: marriage breakdown. This is established if the spouses have lived separate and apart for one year; or if one spouse has committed adultery; or if there has been physical or mental cruelty. Most marriages today are dissolved using the "separate and apart" clause (also referred to as "no fault"). It is less messy, less time-consuming, less costly. Nothing else must be proved. No need for investigations or witnesses. And it doesn't take two to agree that the marriage has ended – one is enough if he or she lives apart. Divorce has been simplified.

Custody is a different matter. All kinds of factors can influence any or all players in the drama – the children, expert witnesses, lawyers, in-laws, judges, parents. All would agree they want the "best" for the children. But that's often where any agreement ends. "I know what's best," is heard from all, "because I am the mother/father/experienced lawyer/judge/expert/child."

While no-fault divorce has made it easier for two adults to part, in some ways it has made disputed custody decisions more difficult. One father, who believes he should have been awarded custody, said, "Now no one cross-examines or finds out the truth about what happened to the marriage." He believes in enforced mediation.

On the other hand, enforced mediation worries some people. They are concerned with protecting an assaulted spouse or child. In these situations, "no fault" doesn't apply – there is justified blame, even if the situation isn't revealed during the divorce hearing.

Loss of custody occurs in so many different ways. Sometimes one parent loses "by default," by not doing anything to stop it. Some parents feel it's simply better for the children to stay with the other parent. Sometimes the children choose which parent they want to live with. Some parents fight until their bank accounts have been exhausted, and lose.

This chapter will introduce you to eight fathers and mothers who started out thinking they would live happily ever after. They may yet live that way, but this chapter will explain how they came to one of the darkest times of their lives: separation, divorce, and breakfasts alone.

John's story

I don't really know what happened. She just went.

When I interviewed John, 43, it was 13 years after he had lost custody of his daughter. A soft-spoken man of few words, he exudes warmth, loves being with children, and is happiest when he is working outdoors. The interview took place in his home, which he and his second wife have renovated. Their two children, six and eight, bounced in periodically from playing outside in the summer sun.

When John's children were born he stayed home full-time to raise them while his wife went out to earn a salary. He readily admits that the decision was made as a result of his losing his first daughter through divorce.

John sees his first daughter for a month every summer and every other Christmas. His life is full and happy; his marriage solid. Even though his daughter is now a teenager, the memory that John will always have with him is that of a three-year-old at the airport reaching for him over her mother's shoulder calling, "Daddy, Daddy! I want you!"

John did not want his five-year marriage to end. He loved his wife. He adored his daughter and had participated in parenting, taking part in diaper-changing, feeding, playing, and late night floor-walking. It had been like that all along, he says. As he puts it, "There were two of us having the baby, not just my wife."

When the little girl was two and a half, his wife left them and moved a few blocks away. John was shocked and baffled by the move. His wife said she needed time and space to "sort out some stuff." John hoped she would do just that, and return home.

He hired a daytime baby sitter for his daughter and entered single parenthood. His wife visited them almost every day during this trial separation, and they lived this way for several months. John says this period was very difficult for him. He wanted the relationship rekindled. His wife didn't.

Then one day his unsuspecting in-laws arrived from out of town for a surprise visit. The visit turned the tide. "I got this phone call at work. They said, 'Hi! We're at the airport, come pick us up.' I phoned my wife and said, 'What do you want to do?' To make a long story short, my wife decided to go back to Quebec with her parents and take our little girl, too."

When I asked how the custody arrangement came about, he took a long time to answer.

"I don't know how the decision was made. I guess I wasn't thinking straight or I'd have tried to get custody then. But with her parents there – I think it was more their idea than hers to leave the province."

John simply didn't know what to do. His wife wanted the marriage to end; John didn't. He felt that given time and patience, perhaps they could get back together. John's in-laws felt the situation was intolerable. They thought that no child should be without its mother, no marriage should be forced to work, no daughter of theirs should live unhappily. With their encouragement, John's wife went home to mother.

John had three strikes against him. In those days, it was "normal" for a woman to keep the children with her; even now, most of the time, the children live with their mothers. Second, he was still spinning from the initial separation. Third, he felt completely alone. In his mind, he was standing by himself and he felt weak, confused, and hurt. His wife had strong allies standing with her.

John didn't rely on his friends for help either. He lived in a small town, where, it seemed to him, everyone was either married or single. If he knew divorced or separated people, he wasn't aware of their situation. He thinks that during the 1970s, divorce had more stigma attached to it than it does now. He was ashamed and heartbroken.

John's daughter moved thousands of miles, and several hundred dollars' plane fare, away from him.

Three months after the visit from his in-laws, John quit his job, rented out his house, and flew to see his wife and daughter in an attempt to reconcile. He stayed a month, but in the end faced the fact that it was over. He returned home to begin his grieving in earnest.

John's contact with his daughter formed a pattern of periodic phone calls, summer holidays, and part of the Christmas holidays. The mother and daughter moved often from province to province and spent some time in the United States. John says that he always knew where they were and where to send the maintenance checks. When it was his time to visit with his daughter, he flew to wherever she lived, picked her up at the airport, and delivered her back at the end of the holiday.

Soon after the separation, John's wife joined a religious cult. His daughter, now 16, knows no other way of life, and is unlikely to.

John first suspected that there was something unusual about her religion when she was eight or nine years old and refused to answer questions about it. The bits and pieces of information he was able to get during summer and Christmas holidays made him nervous; the research he subsequently did into the cult alarmed him further.

At that time, John hired a lawyer and took his daughter to a medical doctor and a psychiatrist, but he feels that experience and information about deprogramming in Canada at that time was limited. There wasn't enough "wrong" with his daughter to make a case to change custody. John was advised to forget it.

Over the next seven years he tried to dismiss the idea of getting custody, and except for the area of religion, his daughter seemed happy enough to visit and share her father's new life on a semiannual basis.

After living with her mother for 13 years, however, his daughter suddenly decided she wanted to live with her father, his new wife, and their two young children. John's second wife explains:

"We'd given up hoping that one day she'd live with us, then out of the blue she called and within a week she was here. We were thrilled to have this chance. What we didn't realize was that she trying to break out of the cult. We didn't know that, didn't understand the implications. It was only at the end, after six months, when she said she wanted to go back home that we understood. She said, 'I just can't make it without the group.' And it was too late. She was going back.

"We saw a counselor – the leaving was traumatic – and arranged for her to see him, too.

"He told us that talking to her was like dealing with fingers that were all threaded through her head – you can't touch them and pull them off because they're too slippery. He said she'd been very well trained and had an answer for everything. He said she's so much a member of that cult that it would take years for her break away.

"John said, 'I think she's gone now. We may see her, but I'll never feel the same way about her.' He was so hurt and so hurt for me, it was all bundled up. At first it came out as anger and then as hurt. We'd tried so hard, but she'd gone."

John doesn't think it's possible for his daughter to break away from the cult. "With adults, at least when they're deprogrammed, there's something to go back to. Not with kids. If you take that away, there's nothing. It's not that it seems to have done outwardly bad things, she seems to be well adjusted, lots of good social skills, is a nice girl. But there's this thing that controls her. It's hard for me to talk about it."

I asked John if he was angry with his daughter.

"No. Any anger or frustration is against the cult, not her. Or against her mother for getting involved. It's not at her. She doesn't have control over what she's doing. Maybe that's a cop-out, I don't know.

"When we parted this last time, it was one of the most emotional partings we've had since the first one, because I think I feel that I don't have a daughter anymore who can think for herself. She's not in control of her own life. That's very hard for me to accept. I think I'll always have a lot of guilt and anger – anger toward the cult and guilt because I didn't put my foot down at first and prevent all that from happening to her.

"When my wife decided to move back to Quebec with our daughter, I should have gone to a lawyer to try to gain custody. It would have made a lot of difference in her life. I'll always feel guilty about that."

John lost his daughter not once, but twice.

Ann's story

I never, ever thought I'd be without my kids.

Ann's 14-year marriage ended when she was 33, while she was in her final year of postgraduate studies at a university.

Ann is an enthusiastic person with an easy laugh and eyes that say she loves life. It is a surprise to discover that she has faced the isolation and trauma of living far away from her children.

The marriage died a natural death, she said. There was no huge explosion, just a fizzle. "We dated early, married young, and grew in opposite directions. Eventually there was nothing there."

When Ann decided she could no longer face the vacuum that her marriage had become, she moved out and established a second home close to her husband's. Their four children were 13, 11, nine, and seven.

With the help of a counselor, Ann and her husband had been working out a system of shared parenting so that the children would have easy and frequent access to both of them.

"We separated in July. During the week, I'd go to the house we'd lived in and take care of the children after he left for work. Then I would leave and he'd stay with them at night. On weekends, we'd alternate. He'd be with them one weekend and the next they'd come to my place.

"Labor Day weekend just before school started was his. For two or three days I wasn't around. I went over on Tuesday and the house was vacant. There was not a stick of furniture left, no bikes on the lawn, no curtains on the windows, no children. He'd kidnapped them. A neighbor kid said they'd moved back to where we'd lived before.

"It was a shock. And I felt betrayed by my brother and sister-in-law who had helped them move."

The week before, Ann's brother had visited her and tried to convince her to return to the marriage. He'd become violent in his effort to convince. Ann explains her brother's reasoning:

"If my family helped my husband and our kids move back to our home town in another province, helped with the 'poor motherless waifs' and gave him a job, I'd have to give up my studies and move back there because I couldn't stand being away from my kids. So I had to make a decision. And there really wasn't any decision to be made. You can't just make a relationship happen. I couldn't move back to a relationship that wasn't there, even if it meant being apart from my kids."

Ann called her lawyer right away and began legal proceedings to try to regain custody. Her energies were entirely focused on this one thing.

She was in her last year at school. Until the term started, she helped the secretaries staple papers together and do other simple jobs, just to maintain her sanity.

Ann found it hard to get up in the morning; she remembers it being difficult to go up and down stairs. Ahead of her loomed the court hearing.

"I didn't know if my husband was going to be there or not. Facing him and the whole situation and wondering what the courts were going to say was very traumatic.

"It was helpful for me that the secretary at the school went to court with me. She'd been separated and knew what it was about so offered to come along. The lawyer was very understanding and that was somewhat supportive."

Because Ann's husband was a competent father and the children had returned to their former home and were surrounded by extended family, the judge ruled in favor of her husband.

Ann had been preparing for the end of her marriage and for a different relationship with her children. She had had no idea that she should have been preparing to live completely alone.

Ron's story

When I first had kids there was a commercial on television. Do you remember it? It said, "It's ten o'clock – do you know where your children are?" I used to think how sad it was they'd have to do that. I was always going to know.
And now, I don't know.

Ron is a construction worker, 35 years old. He arrived for the interview at the exact hour with an oversize briefcase full of photocopied documents, divorce material, briefs, custody cases, and carbon copies of correspondence with his lawyer and his estranged wife. He appears to have documentation for his entire life over the 18 months he was separated from his wife of ten years and his children, aged five and nine. It is apparent that Ron wants never to be caught unaware again. I had asked for 90 minutes of his time. When the hour and 30 minutes had passed, the alarm on his wristwatch sounded. Ron is very precise.

He speaks easily, with little prompting, as if he has told his story many, many times.

Ron and his wife had been childhood sweethearts, dating since they were 16. His in-laws had always been protective of their daughter and involved in her marriage. Ron says he always accepted that circumstance. Ron describes his marriage as "Okay."

"We had good times and bad times, just like anyone else," he says. He maintains that his wife was overanxious about the children and it was two years before the couple went out and left their first-born with a baby sitter (Ron's mother-in-law). Ron remembers that his wife sometimes cried when she had to leave the children and phoned home frequently when they were out.

Ron was at work when it happened. He was on the four-till-midnight shift and came home one night to find his son, daughter, and wife missing. He phoned around and found them at his in-laws' house. He was told his wife had checked herself into the hospital because she was having what appeared to be an emotional breakdown. His mother-in-law explained that everything was being taken care of, that his wife was now with her and sleeping, but that she thought her daughter needed time to sort things out.

Ron accepted the explanation, hung up the phone, and went to bed. He didn't realize that the wheels were in motion for the greatest loss of his life.

Over the next few days Ron was told by both his in-laws and his wife that she needed time and space and was having tests done at the hospital. Ron is unclear just what these tests were. When he visited, he found the children unusually quiet and, although he was concerned, he didn't know what to do. "I took a job out of town for a month until things straightened out," he says.

Ron knew that things were "not right." But when he questioned his wife or her parents, the only answer he got was that she needed time. "However," he says, "it was also quite obvious to me that I was being held accountable for my wife's emotional condition."

Ron's son, aged seven at the time, enrolled in a school near his grandparents' home. Ron said, "It's funny, all those steps were being taken and I was just sitting back, trying to get a grip on the whole thing.

"I was very unchallenging of the whole situation," he says. "There was friction there that I didn't understand. My head told me something wasn't right, but my heart said leave it alone. In the back of my mind I thought things shouldn't be going this way, I should be keeping the kids at home, making some arrangements for them, looking into this on my own...there's more to this than meets the eye."

When the month passed and Ron was back in town, he attempted to talk with his wife and straighten things out. It didn't work. He then tried to arrange mediation counseling to open communication. At that time, he still had hope that this was a "bad patch" in the marriage that would pass. His wife found fault with a series of counselors and refused to participate. Communication between the two broke down entirely.

The death of the marriage was long, drawn-out, miserable. Even when he accepted that his wife no longer loved him, Ron felt they should stay together for the sake of the children. His wife disagreed. Ron didn't make an issue of things for fear of alienating her further, but it didn't help.

Six months after his wife moved into her parents' home, she and the children moved into their own apartment and began a new life. Ron still wanted to be a part of it. He felt he should be able to drop in on his children at any time.

The idea of having regular visiting hours with his children was repugnant to him; he didn't want to put his children (or his fathering) on a time schedule. Parenting, he says, should take place anytime or anywhere.

His wife felt differently. For Ron to "just pop over" seemed to be an invasion of her privacy. She told him it's difficult to get on with building a new life if the old life is liable to turn up at any time.

Ron is beginning to accept this, not because he wants to, but because his attempts to visit the children on his irregular schedule have been consistently sabotaged. His wife was out. Her phone number was changed. His phone calls were not returned, nor were his letters answered.

Ron pushed for mediation again, but two issues have made the exercise a consistent failure. One is Ron's unrelenting (until recently) failure to agree to a set schedule for visits. The other is that at the moment, his wife has what she wants: separation from Ron and sole custody of the children.

When I interviewed Ron, he hadn't had an actual visit with the children for three months. He was maintaining contact with them by going to their school.

"It's great when I see them. My son will run up and put his arms around me. But as soon as his mother comes along, he looks back and forth between us and is very uncomfortable.

"I thought being a parent was being a parent. The marriage was to my wife, but my relationship with my children is independent of that. The marriage, separation, or divorce shouldn't interfere with that relationship with the children."

Ron wants joint custody so the children can spend half their time with each parent. His wife is fighting this. Part of the problem, Ron says, is that he is fighting sexual discrimination. He feels he has to convince the lawyers of the value of the male parent.

"I hear too much from the media and professionals about fathers who don't care," he says. "Well, I'm a father who *does* care!"

It is now up to the courts to decide if Ron will have an opportunity to be half-time single parent, and if two children, aged nine and five, will be able to spend 50 percent of their time with a father who loves them very much.

Peter's story

They said I wasn't fostering shared parenting.

Peter is 32 years old, an elementary school teacher. Unlike the other people I interviewed, Peter was new at the business of living alone. He had been without his children only two weeks. The wound was very fresh. I met Peter in a restaurant to hear about his emotional roller coaster ride.

Peter contends he is a good and loving father and that he was a participating parent and husband. His ideas about shared parenting and shared housework were ingrained in him when he was very young. He is the eldest of eight children.

"When I was growing up on the farm," he said, "I used to see my mother working long, hard hours. My father worked hard, too, and I helped them both. But I remember two particular scenes from my youth.

"One is of my father learning against the pigpen having a smoke and contemplating the sale of his prize hogs. Sometimes he'd stand there for an hour.

"Another is of my mother on her hands and knees washing the floor. Dad would be sitting in the kitchen reading the paper and she'd have to ask him to move his feet so she could wash under them. I didn't think it was fair."

It was Peter's wife, he says, who decided that the marriage had ended. They attended counseling sessions for several months, but she was unsatisfied with the marriage. Her parting words to him were, "You can raise the children. You're a good father."

For six months, Peter was a single parent. He says he was devastated by the marriage failure, but comforted by the fact that the children, aged two and four, were with him. Although they attempted a brief reconciliation, his wife left again. This time, she wanted sole custody. It is Peter's belief that his wife changed her mind for two reasons: she missed the children and resented the artificiality of her visits with them. Furthermore, she had established herself in a home, had a new partner, and was now employed. Twice she took Peter to court in an effort to gain custody. Twice she failed. Eighteen months after the initial separation they were in court again. This time, she won.

A court-appointed social worker had become involved the third time. Peter, dissatisfied with his assessment, arranged to have a psychologist do a home study as well. The psychologist spent a total of 90 minutes with Peter and his children. He found no evidence that Peter was not a good parent.

The lawyer told him that if it appears that one parent is discouraging visiting rights, the judge may give custody to the other parent. "She had nothing else," he says. "There was no wife battering, child abuse, alcoholism, nothing like that. And I was a good father. She knew that.

"I really believed I was up against a giant. I'd heard that in over 80 percent of cases involving young children the wife gets the kids. She knew she had an advantage there. It was her sex.

"There were little things, and for two years I got these blown-up versions of things I had done, my lawyer saying she says you've done this and that. What she was really saying was this guy's being an idiot. He's not fostering shared parenting. It didn't matter what I tried to do, it was twisted around."

Every time an allegation was made, lawyers were involved, even if it was just a phone call. Each time it cost money. By the time Peter lost his case, he had also lost $12,000.

One of the "little things" involved his wife's visits with the children.

"She would pick up the children between 5:00 and 7:00. I would ask her to be more specific, but it didn't work. One time I had a doctor's appointment for 7:00. I waited until 7:15 then left, leaving her a note on the door. I told her where we'd be. But she claimed I was sabotaging her visiting time.

"Just because I'm a father, just because of my sex, doesn't mean I don't feel the way a woman would feel if she was going through this."

Peter felt he was on trial from the moment his wife first sued for custody. The trial, at least, is over. The adjustment is just beginning.

Rose's story

When I think about it now, it's got to be a movie
or a book I read. I can't believe it was my life.

Rose is 42, a receptionist for a small company. I interviewed her in the kitchen of her country home just before Thanksgiving. She was ready for me. On the table was her open photo album with the few photos she has of her three young children; several more recent photos show Rose standing with three young adults. The leap is hard to fathom.

Set up on a stool was a tape recorder so I could hear the children, aged two and four, singing and talking. She also had ready some precious handmade gifts the children had given her a decade ago. She began talking immediately. Two hours later, she asked if I'd like some coffee.

Rose says that her husband swept her off her feet. She had been a shy teenager, ashamed of her grandfather's and father's drinking. At age 20 she met her husband and after six weeks agreed to marry him.

Rose and her husband moved to his small town. She was new and lonely. Her husband drank too much, and frightened and belittled her. Among his friends were the one lawyer in town, the police, the minister, and the priest. The town became a terrifying trap for Rose. She had no one to turn to.

Rose felt she couldn't do anything right, but she tried. She tried to love her husband because she'd married him. She tried to care for their three children because she loved them.

"When you're told and feel that you're good for nothing all your life, you believe it," she says. "I've had to deal with alcoholism all my life; I thought it's what I deserved."

When the drinking and the loneliness and bullying became too much to bear, Rose made one abortive attempt to get away.

"I left the first time in the spring. I contacted legal aid for help, but they told me that in order to get the children, I would have to go through the courts. The older kids [then nine and seven] would have to appear. I just couldn't put them through it.

"All the time I was away [about two months] I got phone calls from my mother. She kept saying, 'Go back home. How can you do that? You've scared the children.' And I was missing them so much and wondering what I was going to do. Then a parcel came with no note or anything, just pictures of the kids. I knew I had to go back. I couldn't live without the kids. No matter what, I had to go back for their sakes."

Rose phoned her husband and he picked her up with plans for the two of them to "start again" in a motel.

"That was the beginning of a whole weekend of rape," she says.

When Rose was finally reunited with the children, her husband forced her to get down on her knees and promise them she'd never leave them again. He told her that if she left and took the kids, he'd kill her. Things changed after that. They got worse.

Her husband no longer went out to drink; he did it at home. He told her he'd been to a lawyer and had legal custody of the children. Her sister-in-law was posted as "guard" to ensure she didn't try to leave with the children. An extension phone was installed to monitor phone calls. And always, always, he threatened to take the children away from her if she made any attempt to spirit them away. It was the worst threat of all – as if he was saying, "Because you already feel guilty about not loving me, I will use my power to take away the people you *do* love." He kept guns in the house. He had a bad temper. Rose was afraid.

Rose relives the second and final time she left as she tells me about it a decade later.

"One Saturday about two months after my return, I knew I had to get out. I couldn't survive another night in the house. We had supper and I tried to act normal. I wanted so badly to tell somebody I was leaving – I almost told him!"

He was going out for the evening with their nine-year-old son.

"My son came up behind me and said, 'Mommy, bend down.' And he put his arms around me and said, 'Mommy, I love you.' And I said, 'I love you, too,' and he said, 'Goodbye, Mom.' And I thought, 'Oh God, why are you doing this to me?' Any other time, if a kid's going out to play, he goes out the door and maybe says bye. It was as if he sensed something.

"My husband told me to have snacks ready because he was bringing some guys back around nine. They had just left and I saw his cigarettes on the table and thought, 'He'll be back for them.' So I sent our seven-year-old over on her bike. Then she came home. You can never get the kids in to get ready for bed if they're out playing, and I wanted to pack some clothes. But when she came back, she came in. I put the girls in a bubble bath to keep them happy and then a neighbor dropped in."

The neighbor, unknown to Rose, was involved with her husband and would later marry him and mother Rose's children. Rose told the neighbor she was leaving. The neighbor canceled Rose's baby sitter and offered to baby-sit that night. Rose stuffed her clothes, a few photos, and some gifts the children had made for her into a garbage bag and set it outside on the steps. She had arranged for a friend to drive her to the next town. From there she planned to take the bus to friends who were waiting for her in another province.

The half-hour bubble bath that the children usually had lasted only five minutes. The children followed Rose around the house giggling. "It couldn't have been harder," she says.

"My friend arrived and I was starting downstairs and I went to pieces. My daughter said, 'Don't cry, Daddy's not at the bar.' And I told her I had a headache and she suggested I go to the drugstore for some Aspirin and I said that's what I'd do.

"So it really bothers me, hurts me, that the last thing I said to the kids for years was a lie. That I'm going to get an Aspirin? For nine years?

"The girls went inside and I looked through the window one last time. Then I got into the van and lay down on the floor in the back."

For Rose, there was never a question of custody. Only survival.

Carole's story

So far, I've been in and out of court for six years. The civil law doesn't apply to poor people. I don't have a chance.

I interviewed 42-year-old Carole in her small, city apartment. A large painting dominated the living room. It depicts a Native Indian woman and her son. Carole explained that the woman in the picture lived in the sky and had lost her son through magic.

Carole was 30 years old when she married. She had known her husband three months. Previously married, he had half-time custody of his three-year-old daughter. Carole was first beaten when she was six months pregnant with their son.

"I find it very hard to forgive myself for not leaving him then. The hook was his little girl. We'd had a custody battle for her and she was really attached to me. Basically, I guess, I was always trying to earn his love. I wanted so much for us to be a happy family."

Five years after the wedding, Carole took the children to a women's shelter and laid common assault charges against their father. He was evicted from the family home and she and the children returned to it. But the story didn't end there.

Five years after the initial separation, Carole still rides a nightmarish merry-go-round. Her charges were met with countercharges. For her "sin" of leaving him, Carole's husband threatened that he would see her in a mental institution or dead from suicide within two years.

Carole's health failed; she required two corneal transplants to prevent blindness. This vivacious mother has a lot to say about the legal and welfare systems.

"The legal battering is worse than the physical battering. People have said, 'You put up with physical abuse for five years!' But the legal and societal battering and the poverty and having to document my stability for the court – those have been infinitely worse than the physical battering."

During the time Carole had the children as a single parent, her husband kept up a steady barrage of allegations of child and sexual abuse. Although there was some financial support at the beginning, it didn't last. Carole was forced to move out of the marital home, sell her major appliances and some furniture, and move to a number of apartments. There were constant legal as well as financial wranglings.

In addition, she was subjected to two psychiatric tests. After an interview lasting less than two hours, a psychologist labeled her psychotic.

In spite of all this, she believes that the kids were happy when they were with her. "I did everything in my power to give a good example and foster a good relationship between them and their father. I'd been reading a lot about children and divorce, and I felt a decent person helps foster a good relationship with the other parent. But the minute he got them, he tried to sabotage our relationship."

Carole spent the week before Christmas preparing for, or attending court. The trial ended on a Friday, two hours before her daughter was to appear in a Christmas concert. The judge ordered the children returned to their father for interim custody. It was more than a year after the separation.

"I got back from court and I didn't have time to give the kids a decent supper before it was time for the concert. I was in a state of shock. I was to provide the kids with adequate clothing, but I'd been in court all week and didn't have the laundry done. I packed what I had.

"I dropped off my daughter at the concert and took my son across the street to Sears. It took the last few cents I had to buy him some jeans and a tee shirt and socks because I didn't want them to say I hadn't provided adequate clothing. I had their clothes in two green garbage bags. I had luggage, but I didn't know if I'd get it back or not.

"He said he'd pick up the kids at 9:00 after the concert. Everyone left the school. The doors were locked, the lights were off. I was standing on the dark steps with two garbage bags and my kids, and I didn't want to cry and upset the children. I was scared because there was no one around."

Carole lost custody because she was labeled psychotic. She said she was numb for a while. Next came a brief period of dreaming about flight. Like other parents facing this challenge, she considered changing her identity, moving to Australia, just getting away. But a friend asked, "Why would you do that to us? Why punish us and the kids by disappearing?"

Eventually, Carole threw out the flight idea and adopted a fighting stance instead. She sought out others who had been in her situation and formed a group. She has set out to try to remake a system that reinforces the hatred in divorce. "The law is set up to destroy one parent," she says. "Winners and losers."

Twice each month, Carole boards a bus and travels four hours for a short visit with her children.

Graham's story

One major thing was separating the furniture.
It was really the only successful negotiation we had.

Graham, a 35-year-old university professor, lives in a townhouse that is a curious combination of bachelor pad and children's art festival. Interspersed with Canadiana pine furniture, an extensive library, and collected art, are bright poster-paint renderings by his children. On one wall, the paintings reach from floor to ceiling.

Graham's description of his early marriage sounds like the ideal that women's magazines are always talking about: equality of the sexes, shared childcare, a sensitive man, and an achieving woman.

"The first year of each child's life we had each been home half-time," he says.

Graham recalls that there had been problems in the marriage for some time and that he and his wife spent the last three years of their 11-year union in marriage counseling. Their children are seven and four. Graham has been separated for one year.

They both agreed that the marriage wasn't working and talked for months about custody arrangements. In anticipation of the separation, Graham went to court asking for joint custody. He suggested that they set up three homes – his, hers, and the children's – and that the parents would take turns living with the children.

"The judge said a couple of things about my proposal. She referred to it as a bird's nest arrangement. She'd seen this arrangement before and in her experience it always breaks down because the parents end up quarreling about who ate all the food in the fridge.

"She also said that since we were still living together, we effectively had joint custody and there was no need to order it. Therefore, my application was premature. I felt I was in a real box."

Graham had tried to ensure that both he and his wife would have significant roles in raising the children and have enough time allotted to do that.

Graham next suggested joint custody, two homes with the children spending equal time in both. But his wife said the mother's role was the major one. She wanted sole custody.

Graham was feeling suddenly shoved aside. He had never been the kind of father who dropped in on the children for a peck on the cheek before bed; he'd participated in *all* aspects of parenting. He *wanted* to parent.

His wife argued that it would be too hard on the kids to go back and forth. They needed stability and should live in one home. Hers.

Shortly before the separation, Graham says the tension around the house was sky-high. It was awful for everyone. Both parents had agreed the marriage was over. The question was, "Who would leave the matrimonial home?"

"I had the sense of being in a situation of playing psychological chicken," he said. "We were supposed to be thinking about the best interests of the children, but I thought the children were suffering greatly under this arrangement."

Graham decided to move out.

"The day I told my wife, I remember the look on her face. I had the feeling she was thinking she'd outlasted me. I imagined that it was as if her lawyer had said to her, 'If you can get him to leave first…'

"I came home from work the next day and discovered the kids had been told. I was appalled. If there was ever a time we needed to sit down together with the children, this was it."

Graham moved into a townhouse, into a neighborhood chosen especially for the park, playground equipment, and abundance of potential young friends for his son and daughter. The day after he moved he went back to court, again asking for joint custody.

Among other things, his wife's lawyer argued that since in a "normal family" the parenting is usually done by one person and clearly children are not hurt by that, there was no reason to think that children would be adversely affected by a sole custody arrangement.

When the courtroom door finally slammed, Graham had been granted "the formula" – every other weekend and three hours Wednesday evenings. The judge, he says, doesn't believe in joint custody.

Hannah's story

It was better this way.
I didn't want the kids to lose their home, too.

Hannah is 42 years old. Although she has never worked in interior decorating and design, it is evident that she has an artistic eye. Her newly renovated home looks like a *Better Homes and Gardens* spread. It, and she, exude charm and warmth. Hannah also has a delightful sense of humor. It helped carry her through the past five dark and lonely years.

Hannah married right after high school and became a mother soon after. She loved the role. She had been a city girl, but adapted to life on the farm with youthful enthusiasm. She worked alongside her husband on the farm and managed an efficient household. She had three children by the time she was 25. Everyone in the family was busy with community activities, children's activities, and work – perhaps too busy. Or perhaps because they had married so young, they outgrew each other. Or perhaps they felt they'd taken on too many adult responsibilities too soon. Or perhaps they never really learned to communicate. Who can pinpoint the day that Apathy becomes a third partner in a marriage? Hannah said she couldn't.

Somewhere along the line the marriage gave a last gasp and died. Hannah heard it, but her husband didn't. Basically, he kept busy. Around and around went Hannah, trying to find happiness in an increasingly empty marriage. Then she fell in love with another man. The situation was against everything in her – her beliefs, her upbringing. But the love she felt only brought to a head all the festering frustration and loneliness she was feeling inside the marriage. Hannah's guilt grew like a weed.

At first she wanted to run away from the love. She suggested to her husband that they move, begin again somewhere else. But they stayed on the farm. Hannah saw a psychologist for a year, trying to get help in deciding what to do, and later, how to end the 20-year marriage.

When I asked Hannah what thoughts she'd had about her children before she left, she said she hadn't known what to do.

"Staying together for the sake of the children" may have seemed the only alternative in the previous generation, but, for better or for worse, it isn't anymore. Part of the reason for this may be that children of those marriages have said quite plainly that it wasn't appreciated. That growing up in a relaxed single-parent family would have been preferable to growing up in a household with loud silences, or bitter arguments, or outright violence.

Hannah realized that her dilemma wasn't whether to stay in or leave a loveless marriage. It was how to leave with the least horror befalling the children. She worried about how they would react. She thought they'd be embarrassed and griefstricken.

"They'd been on the farm all their lives, all their friends were around there, their schools were there. My husband wasn't the best parent, but he wasn't a bad one, either."

In the end, Hannah decided that the most sensible thing to do was to leave by herself.

"But I had always done everything for the children. In fact, when I left I said I'd come back and do things for the kids, but my husband said that was crazy. 'If you're going to leave, then leave!' he said."

Hannah knew her mother loved her, but she also knew that her mother disapproved of her lover.

"Mom kept telling me to stay together for the sake of the children. She saw how unhappy I was, but she thought if I could just get my lover out of my mind it would be all right. But it wasn't just him. I was so unhappy."

Hannah's husband responded to the imminent end of their marriage with bitterness and rage. He talked about his wife's infidelity to anyone who would listen – friends, family, neighbors – including, of course, the children. Hannah was the "fallen woman."

"I remember a visit from my daughter," Hannah says. "She was 16 at the time of the separation. I was beginning to feel that the kids were taking sides. And they were on my side.

They could see that their father was acting like an ass. They'd never been close to him. They didn't seem to blame me, but they didn't want it to happen. They wanted things normal. They wanted me back."

Hannah's eldest daughter, 19, was living at home but working full-time before starting university. Her second daughter was 16 and her son 11. It was the 11-year-old who concerned Hannah most.

"I thought it would be fair if the younger ones came to my place [a 25-minute drive to the city] about two days a week and every other weekend. With prodding from the counselor and demands from the older children, my husband reluctantly agreed to that.

"I wasn't at all prepared legally. But I thought I was prepared emotionally for the separation. I wasn't. I fell apart."

Hannah was wise enough to know she wasn't much use to her children or herself in that condition. Back to therapy she went.

"Seeing the psychologist is what got me through," she says. "I saw her for about the first 18 months. She had a lot of common sense. When I thought I was going over the edge, she'd help me put things in perspective. If nothing else, I think what she taught me was to live with the pain, not to run away from it." Her psychologist helped Hannah to start living again.

These stories are painful to tell and painful to read, but I don't believe they are especially unique in our society. You may have lived through one that is similar, or know someone who has. I found no difference between women and men when it came to missing their kids. They all measured 10 on the Richter scale of grief.

3

Guilt, Anger
and Other Demons

*The demons are with us. Denying that they are, will not
make them disappear. No matter who ended the relationship,
no matter how custody was lost, the demons are alive.
Give yourself permission to grieve your loss.
Be tender with yourself.*

One of the first reactions people have when confronted with disaster is denial. Whether it is a doctor saying the illness is terminal or a spouse saying the marriage has terminated, the pain is too big, the emotion too intense, the knowledge too horrible to accept at first. The mind reels, the body rebels, the spirit is shaken.

The way we cope with such disaster will vary. Friends who stand by us, counselors who offer coping strategies and a willing ear, our own experience, and our personality all influence how we live through painful times.

Some of the men and women I interviewed described the initial reaction as shock. Others talked about "being numb, like at a funeral." Some remember "not thinking straight." It seems no amount of preparation is adequate, no warning bells loud enough.

Even parents who have thought for a long time about ending their marriage are surprised by the depth of their emotions and the unexpected responses from themselves, their spouses or their children, and some family and friends.

Although some parents who did no planning for the end may not have known it was coming, others blocked the admission that the end had come. C.W. Smith wrote in *Will They Love Me When I Leave?* that he neglected to investigate custody procedures because it would have meant admitting that the divorce would mean something terrible to his children.[1]

There are feelings of failure after a divorce. We started life with a mate in hope, love, and joy and we have found that for one reason or another, the hope, love, and joy have disappeared. We have similar feelings about losing or giving up custody of our children. We started a new human life in love, thinking that we would be with the child from diapers to dating and beyond, yet for any number of reasons that dream dissolved, too. We can rationalize and explain and struggle to understand reasons, but the feeling of failure is there.

The following chapter deals with guilt, anger, and the other negative feelings that slip into bed with us at night. Although ignoring these feelings may work for a time, eventually they will raise their heads in the morning and we will need to face them. It could happen when a new partner says something that "pushes an old button." It could happen when our children demand an explanation of us. It could be that we have spiraled into depression and need to face these demons in order to be whole and healthy again.

Fear

Fear plays a large role in the lives of noncustodial parents during the first critical six months of adjustment. Whether they are the "leaver" or the "leavee," they fear many things. They fear rejection by the children. They fear their own incompetence and anger. They fear losing touch with their kids. They fear condemnation by others. Some fear for the physical and spiritual safety and well-being of their children or themselves.

Uncontrolled, that fear can do much worse than rob sleep and weight. Out of that fear we sometimes attribute power to the custodial parent, resulting in fear of asking for more time with the children, fear that the plan will be rejected, fear of losing the time that has been allotted.

Fear of the other parent's power was mentioned time and again by interviewees, both male and female. In spite of what the custodial parent says about support money giving power to the noncustodial parent, the parent without the kids feels acutely that the parent with the kids has the power. Part of the fear is not knowing what the parent with custody is saying to the children. Part of it is simply hearing the children refer to "that other place" as home.

Many parents also fear that one day the children may move to another province or city. One father related that nothing makes him feel so helpless or frustrated as that thought.

The fear for some was articulated by the father of teenagers: "I worry about losing touch with them. I worry that we will be strangers. I don't want to be just another adult in my kids' lives. I want them to care how I feel and what I think about life; I want to have a *bearing* on how they live."

Guilt

Most of us fragile human beings carry around some baggage labeled guilt. For some, it would fit nicely into a small handbag; for others, it overflows a large trunk. *The American Heritage Dictionary* defines guilt as "the remorseful awareness of having done something wrong." What person has not done something wrong? None of us starts "from square one" in the matter of feeling guilty.

Dr. Richard Gardner, child psychiatrist and psychoanalyst, writes,

Most parents are significantly guilty about a divorce. They generally appreciate that no matter how much they and their children may benefit from the divorce, the children are still likely to suffer. Perhaps they will suffer less than they would have had the marriage remained intact, but the children will still experience certain deprivations. There is guilt not only over what has gone before...but over what is to come. One has to expect some feelings of guilt. In fact, if a parent does not feel guilty over the divorce (all promises notwithstanding), I would consider there to be a deficiency in the parent's affection for the children and/or an unrealistic understanding of the potentially harmful effects of the divorce on the children.[2]

I found some differences in the guilt expressed by the men and women. The men talked about feeling angry or guilty or frustrated about specific things that had happened. The women seemed to feel most guilty about the entire separation from the children. Even when the men had participated a great deal in the children's lives, they did not seem to share the sense of guilt associated with exclusion from the kids' lives that the women did.

Furthermore, the women seemed more pressured by family (particularly their mothers) and friends to "go back," to move heaven and earth to make the marriage work, and/or to get custody of the children. The result of that kind of pressure is intensified guilt, anger, and frustration.

This difference made sense to me. Men and women have been conditioned to respond to their feelings in different ways. Although in recent years we have become more conscious of the damage done to both sexes by stereotyping, the bitter residue lingers on.

Dr. Gardner believes that parents must come to terms with their own sense of shame and says that if they don't it will have a negative effect on the children. Since this book is about our new relationship with our children, we need to pay attention to this. Recognizing these feelings – giving them a name and a face – is a first step.

Exactly what is it that we feel guilty about? For some, the guilt is associated with the failure of the marriage, the inability to make oneself and one's partner happy the way good old Dick and Jane's family was happy.

For others it's inaction at the time of separation. Such is the case with John. Thirteen years after the separation he looks back on his wife's decision to move back to Quebec with their three-year-old daughter. He says, "I should have gone to a lawyer. I should have put a stop to it and said, 'She's not going and that's that.' I'll always feel guilty about letting her go."

Hannah believes that people who leave a marriage for another person bear an extra burden of guilt. Her marriage had been unhappy for years and she could find no way to fix it. Her husband refused counseling. They foundered. She fell in love with another man.

She suffered a nervous breakdown. The two men met in her hospital room. Her husband tried to kill the man she loved – and almost succeeded. Afterward, when she asked the hospital staff to move her to a room without blood on the walls and the door off the hinges, they refused. She felt they were punishing her, "making her pay." That night she slept in the hall. The next day she discharged herself and went to stay with her mother.

Four years later, still with the man she loves, and with her 20-year-old daughter living with her, she can speak about that period with her head up. But the guilt lies just beneath the surface.

Although Hannah maintains a good relationship with her 15-year-old son, she knows that he heard over and over again the words "abandoned child." He must conclude, Hannah thinks, that an abandoned child is an unloved child. She feels guilty about this. "We are told from day one that the mother is the anchor of the family. The ultimate sin is to leave. I left."

Helplessness

Current books on divorce talk much about the demons that visit the other victims of divorce – the children. The custodial parent has the advantage of being there to help. He or she can reassure the child, speak to the teachers, make such-and-such allowances for difficult behavior. Parents without kids, particularly those at a distance, particularly those without a history of parental coop-eration, can only guess at what is really going on.

Aside from all the other specific guilt, the big one for all noncustodial parents is simply not being there. This is the agony that robs sleep and stops us in mid-sentence. How are they *really*? What is happening inside them? Is someone being nasty on the playground? Did they fail a test? Do they have the flu? Are they crying into a pillow tonight? Are they experimenting with drugs, alcohol, sex? Who are their friends?

One parent told me about midnight phone calls from her 11-year-old son saying that he was alone. On top of the fear and concern and anger a call like that can generate, there is also the guilt about being somewhere other than at home with that child. The noncustodial parent feels helpless, shut out.

Another parent told me about phoning her teenaged kids one weekend. It was hard to have a conversation since there was a party going on. Yes, there were lots of friends over. No, the other parent wasn't home. Yes, they were having a great time. "Gotta go now!" The distance seems so overwhelming, the dial tone so loud.

Loss of authority

Loss of control over a child is something that begins during the "terrible twos" and escalates throughout childhood. Certainly the beginning of school is one point at which parents realize their input is becoming less important to a child as he or she weighs their words against the wisdom of the teacher, the Cub leader, friends, the family dog. Adolescence is the traditional time when kids try to establish themselves as separate from their parents.

Within an intact family, the parent naturally loses authority as the child becomes more independent, but the child and parent adjust along the way. The changes may be stormy for a while, but then become part of the routine. It is a gradual process.

Parents without kids lose their authority once the door closes. "I don't have to mind you anymore, I don't live with you!" some parents hear. It's a logical outcome of not living with one's children, but it sneaks up on the heart just the same.

Loss of authority over or responsibility for a child is part of the nightmare. Parents have been programmed to answer children's needs. Not doing it – even if the children are well cared for by someone else, even if the child does not go without – takes getting used to.

Another parent admitted that she didn't want her kids "growing up like him." It isn't just authority and responsibility that are lost, but influence as well. We wonder: Will I still matter to my children? Will they be concerned about issues I think are important?

Anxiety about the future

A significant number of men and women talked about the future. Ron worries that by the time his children are adolescents they will have grown away from him. Perhaps this is one of the reasons he finds setting up a *schedule* to visit his own children so repugnant. He fears that when they need him most he'll have been so shut out of their lives by the enforced two week-ends per month that they will not turn to him.

Three of the women talked about becoming grandmothers. All of their ex-husbands have remarried. All of them "felt okay" about that, one expressing the feeling that she was glad the children were receiving extra love and attention. But all worried that the stepmothers would be regarded as grandmothers and that they wouldn't have a role. Which mother would be called if anything goes wrong? Which mother will be at the hospital? Which mother will be called Grandma?

Anger

No matter how the marriage ended and no matter how custody of the children was lost, angry feelings are part of the picture. Everyone is angry. As well as dealing with our own anger, we must try to help our children deal with theirs. Completing the angry scene is the custodial parent's anger. While it is true that we can only control our own anger, we are deeply affected by, and may feel partly responsible for, the anger of others.

Many things make the players in this drama angry. Both parents are dealing with the anger left over from the marriage and divorce. Added to that is what happens between them during post-divorce and ongoing childcare. Neither has the corner on the anger market.

The expectations we think society has of us and the anger from the custodial parent, family, friends and children can make us feel defensive and cornered. It is difficult to live with a feeling of failure. We are angry at ourselves, too.

All this is not to say that noncustodial parents must be saints or doormats. But we do need to recognize that we must find a place to put that anger. It is important for kids to learn that many things along the path of life make us angry, but we can deal with anger in an appropriate and healthy manner.

Rejection

While we may still be dealing with the feeling of rejection by our former partner, some feel rejected by the children as well. This might be only a feeling; other times it is a fact. Children may express this by acting out or by being rude, argumentative, and/or critical. Unless they are very young, their presence in your home is an indication of their commitment to you, their parent. Bad behavior when they are with you could be an indication of the war within themselves and their confusion about why they hurt so much. Especially at the beginning of a visit, parents might find themselves looking across the breakfast table at what I call an intimate stranger: this is the person I held and worried about. This is the child I love. I am intimate with this person, the parent thinks. But the eyes that look back are those of someone with whom the bond has broken; they are the eyes of a stranger.

One father whose wife won custody after a long court battle recounted that his daughter was content with the decision and rationalized the limited time she had with her dad this way: "I think boys are stronger than girls. I think girls are more fragile," she said. "When I'm with you, Mom cries all the time. I think when I'm with Mom you don't cry all the time." This father reasoned that his daughter saw her mother as the one who needed her more.

Sometimes custody is decided by older children or teenagers. This could happen at the time of separation or any time afterward. There are many reasons kids make their choices, and it is important to try to recall one's own turbulent teenage years (whether they were spent in a two-parent or one-parent home) to try to understand.

It was helpful for me to reread the diary I kept when I was 13. Although I was raised in a two-parent family and had two sisters and a brother, reading that adolescent outpouring one would have thought I lived entirely alone. Some family members are not mentioned at all; no one was mentioned more than once, and then only if I was angry at him or her. It was good to remember that at that age I was completely self-centered. I was also judgmental, self-righteous, scared, and good at rejecting the people who loved me!

Sometimes teenagers leave one parent because they prefer the geographic location the other parent has chosen. Sometimes the other parent has more money. Sometimes they're curious about how the other parent is doing. Sometimes they feel the other parent needs them more. Sometimes it's "just because."

It's most important to be truthful at this critical time and to remember that this person is a young adult. He or she may not have as much experience of life as we have, but they have *some* and it should be respected.

John says that when his 16-year-old daughter wanted to return to her mother and the religious cult, he was distraught.

"Her intention had been to stay with us until she finished high school. We tried to talk her into staying at least until the end of the year. We offered to send her to her mother's for the Easter break if she would stay. Near the end we were almost trying to bribe her to stay."

John felt he knew what was "best" for his daughter. He also wanted desperately to have a chance at being important to his daughter. Those are not unreasonable feelings. But when he was truly honest with himself, he decided that it was futile to try to keep her.

The temptation to bribe children is strong. Some parents do it almost automatically from the time the children are very young. "If you go potty, you will have my applause, a cookie, a walk in the park. If you clean up your room, you will have your allowance, a hug, an extra half-hour of television."

But what does bribery accomplish in the end? Not much of value. And it's even less valuable to a young woman or a young man trying to come to terms with life.

Whatever the reason for the decision, the "left" parent's feelings of inadequacy, rejection, hurt, and perhaps anger surface like a painful, ugly boil. The important thing to remember is that the child is trying to act out his or her best interests.

Loneliness

For parents without kids, loneliness is twofold. To parents accustomed to kids and their friends roaring through the house, incessant teenage phone calls, bathroom lineups, and snacks at all hours, a quiet, tidy house seems unreal. All the clean dishes, neatly placed where they belong in the cupboard, seem strange and unnatural. This is the loneliness of many who suddenly find themselves living alone.

Peter, who has only been separated from his children a short time, says, "When I lost my wife, it was tough. It was the hardest thing I'd gone through in my life; I felt half of me was going. But losing the children is worse.

"My wife was always her own person in her own right – she was from a different family. But my children are part of me. Sure, they're people in their own right, too, but they are also really part of me. They're made of me.

"When I'd go into the house their little shoes would be there, their toys. Now I come home and it's like a big vacuum."

The other loneliness is the feeling that no one really understands what we are going through.

Rose talks a lot about the loneliness she felt, even surrounded by other people. She felt she was the only woman in the world who had ever left her children.

Even after the people she worked with learned of her "secret," she had a hard time relating to them or to other women. Unmarried or childless women had no more in common with her than married women who joyfully shared their baby's latest antics. The few divorced women Rose knew of had their children with them. She felt unconnected to any of them.

"It would have made it so much easier if I'd known there were support groups for people like me," she said during the interview. "How do I find one now?"

Adding to her complicated situation, Rose wrote letters to her children for months, but they were always returned marked "refused." She continued writing and eventually the letters stopped coming back, but they were unanswered. As she talked about this, her eyes grew wide with the unanswered question, "They *do* want to hear from me, don't they?" she asked.

We are lonely for our kids. We may also find that we are lonely for friends and for the social experiences that were part of family life.

Compounding our attempts to rebuild our lives is the strange phenomenon of being single. We not only struggle to parent at a distance, we are suddenly catapulted back to single status. Although it is common to hear harassed single parents saying that noncustodial parents are now fortunate to be free, this loneliness doesn't feel like good fortune.

John said, "Your whole social thing changes. You're not invited anywhere as a couple or as a family anymore. You don't fit like you used to."

Although Ann was quite busy initially with her postgraduate studies, she also felt the shock of readjustment. "I had to get used to being alone, trying to discover who I was. It was hard. I'd been somebody's wife and somebody's mother most of my adult life."

There are still so many stereotypes. The myths go like this: married people have happy homes and security; single people have their own money, independence. In reality, newly single parents often have poverty, loneliness, insecurity, and doubt.

Society has waited too long to demythologize motherhood, fatherhood, and our understanding of what constitutes a normal family. "Swinging singles" and "happy homemakers" are both stereotypes that have got to go.

Self-condemnation

A friend of Hannah's told her that if our children turn out well, we've had nothing to do with it. If they turn out badly, it's all our fault. Many noncustodial parents buy that myth.

One parent I spoke with said she was grateful her children have gone to university, "even though I wasn't there." Ann is grateful that her children are "healthy, loving, achievers."

Perhaps no parent takes this for granted, but as C. W. Smith writes in *Will They Love Me When I Leave?* "When something goes wrong, we go for the jugular."[3]

Smith relates that his teenaged daughter began taking drugs. Eventually she was hospitalized. He discovered a support group for parents whose children were addicts. He blamed himself and his divorce for his daughter's condition.

Suddenly he realized that the other parents were not all divorced like him. They were single, married, educated, uneducated, rich, poor, and so on. "We divorced people have no corner on the market when it comes to problems with kids," he writes.

"If our children are having problems now, if they have problems in the future, the most sensible response should not be, 'How did I cause this?' but, 'How can I help solve it?'"

New life, new home

Setting up a new home is a perplexing task for parents without kids. Some want reminders of the children everywhere – drawings, photographs, toys. Carole's apartment, for example, is full of reminders that she's a mother – gifts from children, Mother's Day cards, and so on. Like Graham, she's chosen to live in a neighborhood that has lots of exuberant children around. Their calling, yelling, and laughing drifted up through the hot summer air and in through her open windows the evening I interviewed her. It makes her happy, she said.

At first I did not share Carole's feeling about reminders. It seemed the more hurt and vulnerable I was feeling, the fewer reminders I wanted around. At one point I thought about putting anything and everything that said "kid" on it into the spare bedroom and shutting the door. Within a few months, though, that feeling left me and I, too, felt more relaxed about what the kids left when they visited and what memories they evoked. I think it's nice for my children to see those baby pictures on the wall, their artwork, and various paraphernalia around each time they come. It's one more thing they can count on in their topsy-turvy world.

Keeping busy

My sporadic journal entries show that my first six months passed in a busy blur. Three weeks after the separation I was hired to do a job I'd never done before. I was the only reporter on a small weekly newspaper. It was challenging and time-consuming. It not only paid the rent, it kept me working long hours filled to the brim with challenging events and new people. And every week when the paper was printed with my byline in it, my job also told me that I was "good for something." I needed to know that.

Other people talked about "burying themselves in work" to get them through the first painful weeks and months. Graham was working on his dissertation.

"It was good," he said. "It was a project bigger than me. I could walk into the work and lose myself in it. It was the only thing I could do to get away from the situation."

Another parent left nine children because her husband said if she took them he'd kill her. She said that she moved to another province and immediately began working three jobs. Without being exhausted, she said, she would have gone crazy.

Moving forward

It is important to work through our feelings of helplessness and guilt and anger. It is important for ourselves, for our children, and for those who love us now and those who will love us in the future. One man said that he was afraid of his leftover anger from the marriage because he thought it might poison his new marriage.

Others talked about "having their buttons pushed," becoming hurt or resentful or angry out of proportion to the event. They realized that feeling actually came from their past, not from the here and now.

"People who try to avoid the hurt – that's when they go crazy or kill themselves or get into alcohol or drugs," said one mother. "You face the hurt and live through it. If you can just feel the pain and cry or do whatever you do, and know that tomorrow it will still hurt, but it won't be quite so bad – that's what helped me."

Some things we can change: mainly ourselves. We cannot, no matter how determined we are, change the rest of the world – or even the rest of the family.

Brenda Rabkin's book *Loving and Leaving: Why Women Are Walking Out on Marriage* has some wisdom about feeling guilty.[4] Rabkin says if we don't feel guilty we cannot forgive ourselves. If we don't forgive ourselves, we cannot forgive others. These are simple, yet profound words.

Guilt, anger, sadness, and feelings of helplessness are part of the human condition. None of us escapes these feelings, whether we are divorced or married, young or old, male or female. These feelings, though, have a particular manifestation in divorce and custody. If these emotions are too much to handle alone, help may be needed to deal with them. What we must do is recognize these feelings in ourselves, put them in perspective, and move forward, remembering who we are as parents without kids and as human beings.

4

Other People

*If your kids turn out to be murderers and thieves and end
up in prison, it's your fault. If they turn out to be brain
surgeons and lawyers and win the Nobel Prize,
you had nothing to do with it.
You might as well accept that now.
– advice to Hannah*

As if the pain we already feel isn't enough, at the time we feel most vulnerable, we need to deal with others' comments, suggestions and criticisms, too.

Many people who have lost a loved one through death are offered bungled expressions of sympathy. Sometimes they are asked inappropriate questions that can anger or depress. Often it's because the friend is feeling threatened and upset, wondering, "Could (or when will) this terrible thing happen to me?"

People going through a divorce face similar situations. People are curious as well as sympathetic. In a very human effort to understand, and to defend their own partnership perhaps, the same kinds of thoughts are expressed. The least understanding friends are perhaps the ones who feel most threatened by the event. They are defensive of their own situation. Divorce strikes not only the husband and wife and their children, but their extended family and their friends as well.

So it is with loss of custody. It was important for me to remember this when I felt judged by people close to me. I was hurt. I wondered what made them sound so judgmental. I concluded that (a) I was extra sensitive and vulnerable and that

(b) my new status was somewhat threatening to them. I had changed the rules. What were they now? Even I didn't know.

Friends ask, "How can you?"

I was having coffee with a new friend (married, with children) soon after my separation and in the course of the conversation she discovered that I was the mother of three children who lived with their father. Her face registered shock.

"Oh," she exclaimed, "how can you *live* without your children?"

I don't know exactly. You just do. You don't like it, but if you can't change the situation, and if the children are in no danger, that's what you do. Some of us do it with help from a counselor or a therapist. Some of us just muddle along by ourselves.

Another friend of many years wrote me letters stating that she "hoped I would return to the family soon." I knew that she was in deep turmoil about my situation. I waited, hoping that if she couldn't understand she would at least accept a situation she couldn't change. Eventually, I gave up waiting. Each time she wrote I felt a judgment handed down. I felt I'd already been judged. I didn't need her to do it, too. At last I stopped writing to her.

Ann's friends were very vocal when expressing their shock and dismay.

"My family had been so judgmental. They felt that my husband was right – the one who had been wronged by me. I felt judged. They influenced my friends. Sometimes my friends would telephone and say, 'You have to put your family first, that's what God requires of mothers and wives, to put their families first. Give up your studies for the last year and come back at least until Christmas.'

"That kind of pressure was constant. These were the people I'd always looked to for support. I couldn't depend on them anymore. I felt torn apart because they'd been close to me. But my decision couldn't be made on the basis of what my family and friends thought. I started avoiding them, hanging up the phone."

These things happen between friends and families. They can't be expected to fully understand unless they, too, have "been there." No one knows the inside of a marriage or any other intimate situation better than the principal players.

Other people found that their friends were supportive and acted as life lines.

During John's struggle to face each empty day and accept the monumental change of life without his wife and daughter, he found a friend. He moved in with him and his family and says he spent an hour or two every day "just talking." He adds, "I don't think I'd have made it through without him. It happened that he was there and I needed someone to help me get through that."

Another father says he sought out other men facing the same change. "I found myself with friends who were going through the same thing," he says. "I needed them. Night after night I went out. I didn't want to be alone."

For the sake of the children, Dear

Hannah, who had been in therapy for a year to work up the courage to leave her marriage, continued with it for 18 months after the separation. It's what got her through the months of turmoil and the feeling of total rejection by her friends, she says. Also, her sister and brother condemned her, and her mother didn't understand why she couldn't stay "for the sake of the children."

During the final death throes of the marriage Hannah tried telling her mother how she was feeling: "I said to Mom one time, 'I never see him. We haven't sat down together or gone to bed together in I don't know how long. I don't just mean sex; holding hands and having a cup of cocoa together would be nice. There's nothing.'

"And she said, 'Well, it could be worse; he could be gambling.' Our mothers come from a different upbringing. It didn't matter so much about personal happiness, there had to be a reason. If there'd been a *reason*, my leaving would have been acceptable. But because I wasn't happy, that wasn't good enough.

"It was hard for Mom. We'd been married so long and she liked my husband. Eventually she did a lot of listening to me, but she kept saying my husband was a better man than my lover. She'd never met my lover, but she *knew* that. It was two years before she'd meet him." It was Hannah's middle child who eventually forced the issue. She invited her grandma to her mom's house and wouldn't take no for an answer. The first meeting was stiff, but everyone made an effort for the sake of the girl. Subsequent visits have been easier and happier.

Hannah found that allowing her children to talk about their feelings helped clear the air. The first Halloween her older daughter spent a day sewing her little brother's costume; that had been Hannah's job. Her daughter wasn't pleased about having to be a fill-in mom and told Hannah so. Hannah simply listened. Her younger daughter became confused and angry after hours of listening to her father belittle her mother. She, too, was able to verbalize her anger at her mother. Once spoken, the fuse was snuffed out and they were able to discuss their new lives.

Having people make hurtful comments during that time is difficult to say the least. But having them say nothing, look through you, can have the same effect or be worse.

Soon after the separation, Hannah's 20-year-old daughter married. Hannah says that it has been the worst result of the separation.

"She took the easy way out – she got married. She didn't want to move in with me; she felt she was a big girl. She didn't want to continue living with her dad. She was in university at the time, so she didn't have her own money. I guess the marriage proposal came at a time when she was feeling very vulnerable."

For Hannah, the wedding was grim. She was unhappy about the wedding and she was forced into close contact with relatives and friends who disapproved of her.

"I've never been in a room where I was so hated in my life. It's traumatic enough to have your first-born marry. Add to that your disapproval of the wedding and your recent separation from the bride's father. On top of it all, I was in a room full of in-laws who wouldn't talk to me!

"I never had any enemies that I knew about. It's a horrible feeling. I had no self-esteem. I was afraid to say boo to anyone. I felt so bad about myself. It's a vicious circle. You're trying to get on with your life and you can't."

Ann's family *did* abandon her. They helped her husband spirit away the children.

One brother had been physically abusive, and when her other brother was planning to visit her, Ann felt nearly driven to insanity.

"My mother phoned my aunt who lived nearby and asked her to phone and find out if I was actually insane. And I thought, 'Well, if I'm not, I'm going to be because of all this pressure.' At a time like that, you have to put barriers around yourself.

"The only people I could depend on for support in whatever decision I was going to make were the students and professors and my church as a whole. I had a paranoia about my family and friends from my past – about meeting them and rejection by them. It took years before I overcame that."

It took a great deal of patient waiting and careful treading before Ann and her mother were reconciled. Eventually the family accepted Ann again, but for years she felt abandoned.

As in Hannah's story, it was the children who helped their parent and their extended family come together again, simply by example.

Rose and her mother have never reconciled, even after ten years. Her mother can not or will not accept her reasons for leaving (alcoholism and violence) as valid. On one of Rose's children's birthdays, a friend came into church to say there was an urgent message to call her mother. Rose, of course, thought that someone was ill or had died.

"I was really down and out," Rose remembers. "I dialed the number and when she finally answered, I said, 'What's wrong? Did something happen to you or Dad?' And Mom asked me where I'd been. I told her at church, having a mass said for my daughter. She said, 'They let people like you in church? I just called to say it's your daughter's birthday.'

"It's still going on, " Rose says. "My mother's been married for 38 years, but not happily."

Carole says that overall her family has been supportive of her. The one disappointment she has is that neither her mother nor her close friends have ever acknowledged the extent to which she was physically beaten. She doesn't understand it.

"My family doctor took the stand and talked about my bruises, but they will not acknowledge that I was beaten and battered to the extent I was. I guess it's partly my fault. I was hypocritical in that I lived a lie. For years I pretended I was very happy and would wear turtleneck sweaters and long-sleeved shirts if necessary. I feel guilty about that."

She relates a conversation with an older woman about her feelings: "She told me that I wasn't a hypocrite, that I was merely an ordinary woman fighting to save her family and that's what women have been taught to do. I found out later that she had been beaten for 30 years and that she left her husband soon after that conversation."

Carole goes on: "If I was still being physically battered, the kids might not respect me, but they wouldn't respect their father, either. And they wouldn't think I was crazy (as they do now), so it's six of one, half-dozen of the other. The hardest part for me to cope with is society's endorsement of wife beating, society's laissez-faire attitude toward it. And the church's."

One man said his sister was the most supportive. "I don't know how she knew what to do, but she did. We don't even live in the same province, but when I told her what had happened she came through for me. She sent me $150 long-distance gift certificate with a note saying I could call anytime. I certainly did call her, but just knowing that she cared that much made a big difference to me. It was like a safety net that had 'I love you' written on it."

Ex-partners

Some parents without kids must deal with the fact that their child is being served harsh words with the morning porridge by the custodial parent. Angry custodial parents who lean on their children or who regularly spew out their anger and frustration sow seeds of bitterness and bewilderment in the kids.

Children, even those who knew the marriage was a bad one, are usually angry that it is over. They have lost the hope that one day it would improve. That's difficult enough to deal with, without one or the other parent dumping their own anger on the children.

This is one of the most frustrating positions for the noncustodial parent to be in. What to do? Retaliate in kind? Ignore it and keep mum? Calmly answer infinite questions and accusations visit after visit?

In some cases it may be wise to let these secondhand versions of your behavior or personality pass. Other times brief explanations are needed. In either case, respect for the child's bewilderment is important. Your child is watching your reaction. Keeping a cool head and a warm heart may be difficult, but it will be well worth it when the dust settles.

Sometimes corrections are called for. One husband told the children their mother had left the marriage because she was mentally ill as a result of paternal sexual abuse. It was a lie, and she told them it was.

Others I spoke with told similar stories of lies, half-truths, or distorted facts being told to their children. One parent suggested saying calmly, "That's what your mom/dad says, but this is what I know…"

A custodial parent's raging does not automatically mean that a judge will reverse custody. Parents in this situation must once again weigh their financial situation and the horror of subjecting children to yet more stress and anxiety against a *possible* change in living arrangements.

I interviewed one adult child of divorce whose custodial parent had said "terrible things" about her mother. In the end, the daughter said she lost respect for her father. She had always been close to her mother, and while she didn't understand exactly why the marriage failed, the relationship she'd had with her mom held fast.

"We've always had a good relationship," she said. "Mom was always there. I didn't see Dad very often; I guess I didn't know him personally. I'm starting to now, a little, but I just don't get along with him very well.

"When Mom left I really had no one to talk to. I'd really never talked to Dad very much, just 'pass the bread' or something."

I asked her if she felt sorry for her father. She carefully searches her memory, carefully chooses her words.

"He said a bunch of, not lies exactly, but something in between lies and truth. It made me angry that he gave me information I didn't think was true. That was the only time I was really angry."

When one man reluctantly left his marriage, his teenagers told him that his wife was "bad mouthing" him. For two years the boys heard it. During the third year, the oldest asked to move in with his father and his new wife. He couldn't stand listening to it anymore, he said.

All parents would do well to remember that our children are half us and half the other parent. Railing against one parent is like railing against part of the child. It hurts the child to have to listen to it.

The foregoing examples of expressed anger and hostility are one side of the coin. Another side is subtle anger, also directed at the noncustodial parent.

Most people know that separation, especially after a long union, is expensive. One father talks about his young son's analysis of the situation:

"Near the beginning of the separation the kids were getting the poor mom stuff. As far as I can find out, she didn't lay it on, never said much, but they were around her, and they thought she was in a terrible financial situation and that I was doing pretty well. She was always talking about the bills and that sort of thing."

This can be frightening for dependent children. It can also stir up a lot of animosity toward the noncustodial parent. The father didn't want to involve an 11-year-old in their finances, but felt it was the only way to make him understand.

"I got out a pen and paper and just showed him in simple arithmetic however much it was I was going into debt each month. I itemized the things I was paying for and also listed the substantial assets his mother had, as well as her job and mortgage-free house. She was okay, but it took a long time for the kids to realize that."

Sometimes we are so sensitive to the criticism, and so wound up with telling our children we still love them, we almost miss hearing things that can brighten our days immeasurably.

Another father told me that he was driving his children back to their mother's and reassuring them in every way he could think of that he loved them.

"You know I love you, don't you?" he asked. "Yes, Daddy. You tell us that all the time, a thousand times. But do you know I love you?" his daughter responded.

"It was the first indication I had that they might be insecure about my knowledge of their love for me," the father said. "I'd been so worried about their knowledge of my love for them."

The community

By community I mean the people with whom we regularly interact: people at work, play, business, worship; people on our street, at the grocery story, in the law office.

Expanding beyond this circle that envelops each of us is the community that comes to us through television shows, radio programs, books, magazines, and newspapers. As we live in the world, we know that there are certain expectations we have of our companions and that they have certain expectations of us.

In the 1950s, when the "little woman was supposed to stay home and bake cookies in her high heels" while the "little man went out in his fedora to make money," people knew their roles in society.

In the 1990s, not only does Dad change diapers, but Mom earns bigger paychecks than ever before. But the dust from the changes hasn't settled yet. We are still fighting to have women accepted into administrative and management levels in the workplace and men accepted as stay-at-home parents.

We are in a time of social revolution. While women feel they have made some progress, some men feel women have gone too far. The result is a symphony out of sync – and the sound produced is anguish for many men, women, and their children.

Society tells divorcing parents many things: that it doesn't like the divorce; that the children should be with both parents; that each parent should have custody; that women should be home with young children; that women should be independent; that we should have lots of money – and that we should all be happy!

While it is hard enough to weigh what "feels right" for us and our children, we are constantly bombarded with society's expectations. Currently, society expects men to help with childcare and women to be financially independent. What does this mean, though, to families struggling with divorce? What it means to me is that no one knows the answer. Actually, I wonder how many of us even know the questions. And as with the birth of anything significant, it is a painful struggle for all of us.

Gerald, who was 50 when he ended his 25-year marriage, had been a minister in the same town for over 20 years. Although he wasn't actually fired, he "felt it best to leave." He had wanted to stay in the same town in order to be near his 11-year-old son until the boy was older, but two years was all Gerald managed before he moved away.

"In the community, there were people who were really supportive – not in the sense that I could do no wrong, but in the sense of saying, 'He's a human being, the same human being he was before. This has happened. So what? We're not going to reject him.'

"Others were judgmental. They were angry and confused. They wondered how their minister, a leader, could dare to divorce. How dare he do this terrible thing to *them*?

"My children [three of them were young adults] played a supportive role," Gerald explains. "They were sort of stunned at first, but very quickly rallied and became very nonjudgmental. I relied on them.

"They wondered what people expected. They said, 'You've stood by these people through all kinds of situations, some of them very similar.' They thought I was getting a raw deal from the things people were saying."

One woman has found little understanding from society. She left her husband more than 20 years ago when they were overseas. She took her daughters, but left her son, 18 months old. She's never seen him since. Margaret says that although her marriage was terrible, her husband was not a bad father.

"I'd seen all this to-ing and fro-ing of children between their separated parents, and I thought, 'What if I was to be really civilized? What if we made a decision to separate completely?'"

There were many complicating factors involved in her decision: the boy would be safe and well cared for; he looked just like his father; his father was having an affair with Margaret's best friend while she delivered the child.

"I've felt guilty about it, many times," she says. "A lot of people don't know, because it's not a part of my life that they know anything about. Occasionally I choose to tell somebody and there's this incredibly shocked silence. 'How *could* you?'"

She pauses before answering her own question. "Unfortunately, we are sometimes forced to make decisions when we are not equipped," she says quietly.

She keeps her son a secret. Her experience tells her that there is no sympathy and little understanding for what she did.

When I heard her story, I thought immediately about young women who "give up" their babies for adoption. I've never considered that a selfish or thoughtless act. I consider it brave.

People in the community can help. John feels that his involvement in the community served as an antidote to his painful sense of loss.

"I lived in a small town," he said, "and having a job to do and remaining involved in sports and environmental groups helped me see there's another part to life as well. It's not all wrapped up in a little girl who isn't here anymore. You have to keep hold of something, you need something to give you stability."

The groups he belonged to were important. They were not support groups *per se*, but without discussing children or divorce or custody they became supportive for him. The groups valued his participation for who he was – just John.

The legal system

Ron claims that he is having a hard time convincing the legal system that the male parent is important. He feels he is the victim of sexism.

There has been a surge of anger throughout the country in the recent past; men's groups are forming from coast to coast to coast to examine and fight the premise that mothers are the "more natural" or better parent.

While women have been asking their husbands since the 1960s to participate in childcare, when the marriage fails and the men want to continue their parenting, they are being told to back off.

Graham feels cheated by the system and betrayed by his wife. Although his wife wanted a participating, involved father for her children, Graham feels he has been shut out. He, like Ron, feels that he is a victim of sexual discrimination: his parental skills and nurturing nature are not as valued as his wife's simply because he is a man.

Graham has been in a battle for joint custody for the past year. He says his friends agree with him that he should have more time with his children. All agree that this would be best for the children and better for him. Moreover, the children want more time with their dad. But with one exception, all his friends think he should stop the court battle for this right. He's advised to "cut his losses."

Carole's living room contains a large filing cabinet with labels on each drawer: "Custody," "Divorce Cases," "Family Law." She has transformed her anger into action – writing briefs, supporting others, speaking to groups, doing research. Her focus in life is to maintain contact with her children and to do battle for a more just justice system.

What began as Carole's reaction during her first few months of being a childless parent has become a lifelong crusade for children's right of access to their parents.

"Most people do not want to believe how unjust the justice system is. They have to believe that a convicted criminal is guilty and that parents who lose custody of their children are rotten parents. It's like, 'My mind's made up, don't confuse me with the facts.'"

Carole firmly believes that the divorce and custody system we have today is set up to "destroy one parent," and she is frustrated that society needs to believe in the system. "They don't realize how the children are suffering," she says.

Other parents I interviewed agreed with Carole. They don't believe that custody or divorce belong in the court where criminals are brought to justice. In most divorces, there is no "criminal," merely two people who can no longer live together.

In *Listen to Their Tears: How Canadian Divorce Law Abuses Our Children*, Don Peacock describes what he thought when the judge awarded him custody:

In his brief statement he gave me custody of my son. I had won. Though relieved, I had, however, no sense of jubilation.

The whole process had afforded everyone involved three years of needless, nightmarish misery, and I again felt angry to think that we had all been victimized by an indefensible and wholly irrational system."[1]

Peacock's "win" came after he was arrested twice, had spent thousands of dollars on legal fees, quit his job, fled across the country, and had exposed his son to witnessing his arrest. Some win.

In spite of this, society appears to regard his approach to "fighting for his son" as heroic. But refusing to put children through anguish like that exposes that parent to huffy comments such as "what kind of parent could give up a child?"

Ann Landers has commented on custody in her syndicated column. In writing to a mother who gave custody to her ex-husband, Ann said, "Often the mother who gives up custody is performing the most heroic act of her life. Such women deserve praise, not criticism and scorn."[2] The same could be said of such fathers.

Some parents, like Peacock, wage a battle to retain or regain custody. Others said it seemed simpler, less confusing for the children, and more sensible that they leave and have the child or children remain with the other parent. This was sometimes the "main parent," or the parent who kept the matrimonial home, or it may have been the parent who earned more money. Some felt the continuity of schools and familiar neighborhoods would help their children better adjust to the separation.

Throughout many of the interviews, I was reminded of the King Solomon story in the Bible. Two women appeared before him, each claiming that the baby they had with them was their own.

"Cut the living child in half and give half to one and half to the other," the wise ruler ordered.

The first woman stood silent. The second woman begged him not to do it and said, "Let her raise the child, then."

Solomon decided that the real mother was the second one, the woman willing to become a noncustodial mother rather than see the child harmed.

When I feel judged, I remind myself of this story.

I think that when society begins to actively support and accept joint custody arrangements and understands that not everyone can work out shared parenting after divorce, the burden on all members of split families will be less. There are no real winners in a divorce. There are only people who make the best of a sad situation. Friends who stand by us, not because they "pick sides," but because they love us, go a long way in healing some of the hurt. When society stops thinking of us as "bad people," judging by whether or not we "won" the children, we will have made great strides.

5

Waking Up without the Kids on Special Days

"Can you talk about your first Christmas?" I asked.
Silence for a while. Then he said quietly, "I got drunk."

Part of how we manage the first few months in our new life depends on whether or not significant events such as birthdays or Christmas fall within that time. Although those days are always bound to cause some sadness or loneliness, they are more acute if the wound is less than six months old. Not enough scar tissue has grown yet.

My first Easter sneaked up on me. I hadn't prepared for it, hadn't put up barriers or provided myself with cushioning. I'd planned to be with my children for part of the day, but they unexpectedly went away with their father. I was stunned. Rather than phone a friend and say, "Help!" I spent the day alone feeling sorry for myself. I vowed I'd never do that again.

You cannot relive that first special day you spend without the children. It is captured on mental videotape and replayed on the anniversary every 12 months. There are lonely days in between, but on the days you cherish it is very important to take care of yourself. These days seem to last forever. Some people need people and some people need silence on these days. You are the only one who knows yourself.

Rather than have turkey and cranberries turn to ashes in his mouth, one father chose to stay home with a peanut butter sandwich Christmas Day. He had spent Christmas Eve with his children; Christmas Day they were with their mother. Although he was invited to visit friends for the day, he stayed home. He has no regrets.

"I didn't want to pretend. I knew I needed to be alone. I would have been more lonely with a bunch of people, no matter how nice or inclusive they were. You can be lonelier in a crowd than alone sometimes."

Interviewees said that although many of the traditional festivities are difficult, Christmas is the toughest. Perhaps it's because the whole world seems to be celebrating at once and it is in evidence from October to January.

Real Christmas, pretend family

Hannah had been absent from the matrimonial home for about two months by Christmas. She wanted to go to her local Christmas Eve carol service, but because she was involved with another man she didn't want to be seen with him. Not yet. Instead, they drove to a large church an hour away.

She wanted to be there, to celebrate the season, but she felt she'd lost all her friends by ending her marriage and her family was unsure what to think of her.

"When the choir came in singing I knew I was going to cry. I reached into my purse for one of my magic tranquilizers to help me through it, but without a glass of water I began to choke on it. Here I was, worried about crying, and suddenly I knew I had to worry about breathing instead. My sense of humor saved me. I began to laugh at how ridiculous it was."

Hannah delivered gifts the next morning to her three children. "I even took one for my husband. The five of us sat around the tree and opened gifts and it was very uncomfortable. I stayed about an hour and then cried – wailed – all the way home."

The thing that sticks in her mind, four Christmases later, is the feeling she had that hour.

"I kept thinking, 'They're sitting with a mother who doesn't live here anymore, and they still accept me. They must really love me.'"

Hannah's attempt to return to the circle under the tree for a few hours on December 25 wasn't an isolated case. I discovered that several parents, out of a genuine desire to "make it nice for the kids," tried it. One called it "sad, like being in a pretend family." No one said they wanted to try it again.

Graham, who also attempted this kind of first Christmas, remarked on the high tension around the season. "This was a period when we discussed reconciliation. Four months after you separate, sometimes you're not exactly sure what the future will bring, so you're not sure how separated you want to be."

If the family might reunite, Christmas or other family celebrations are a testing ground. Just exactly how do I feel, anyway?

One of the problems seems to be the ritual of opening stockings. In many families, this is done at a certain hour, or after a special breakfast, or when both Mommy and Daddy are up, or whatever. At first, grieving parents have a hard time coming up with a new tradition. Because they feel that the children have gone through so much confusion and uncertainty during the separation, parents are unwilling to change these few precious hours in the year. And so scenes like Graham's "first" Christmas result. He had moved out in September. He and his wife had spent a good deal of time in lawyers' offices and court. The children were three and six.

"We tried to negotiate Christmas. It was awful. She insisted on having the children Christmas Eve and I felt manipulated into trying to recreate the old Christmas, dragging me further and further back in. She wanted me there for Christmas Day. Her sister was coming, too. She invited me over for breakfast and the opening of gifts. The kids would really like that, she said. Then she asked me to come first thing in the morning, 6:30, so I could see them open their stockings.

"I'd made a little wagon for my son and was up until 5:00 in the morning finishing it. I had a shower, lay down for an hour, and then it was time to go over. When I got there, everyone was fast asleep. It was cold, snowy, dark, and there I was, banging on the door."

Graham went through the ritual, which he says felt very, very long. He took the children to his townhouse for the afternoon and then back to his wife's for the traditional turkey dinner. Mutual friends had been invited, too.

"I wouldn't do that again. Everyone seemed to be pretending that everything was normal. I felt it a real strain. When the meal was over, I excused myself. I was relieved it was all over.

"Even though that was the house I'd built and lived in and paid for, I realized when I came back to the townhouse, that this was my home. I was glad to be here, away from the tension."

Carole said her first Christmas wasn't the worst. "There was going to be another trial in May and I understood that he just had interim custody of the kids, so I still had a lot of hope.

"My mother was there and the kids came over during the day. I was in a neighborhood where I felt loved. The neighbors banded together and were very kind. They bought the kids presents and sent over home baking and goodies."

Carole's worst Christmas came two years later. She had become impoverished by poor health and legal fees. To save money, she had moved into the YWCA. Her lawyer warned her, though, that if she wanted to exercise her visiting rights she would need to have more appropriate accommodations.

She had just moved into an apartment expecting to have her children stay with her for part of the school holiday. The week before Christmas she discovered that they'd moved to another city.

"I was in this apartment and had boxes all over the place. Friends insisted I stay with them for Christmas. It was the hardest thing I ever did. I didn't want to go; I just wanted to spend the day by myself and cry. I knew if I didn't go they'd be terribly hurt.

"I remember leaving the festivities at one point and going to call the Helpline. I said, 'I don't want to be here. I should be thankful to have these friends, but I want to be alone and cry and I can't cry because I'm here.'

"They said I should be with my friends, but I said my friends should realize that it would be easier to be alone. I had all these conflicting emotions."

Mother's Day

Dreading a particular day or event isn't much use to anyone. On the other hand, planning for it can reap unexpected results.

When I was a child, Mother's Day was very special. We all went to church and then packed a lunch and headed for our first picnic of the year in the woods to see if the trilliums and wild violets were out.

When I became a mother, Mother's Day was generally disappointing. I was always looking for something that wasn't there. Unfortunately, May was usually a very busy month for my husband and I was let down. When the marriage ended, I buried the hope that Mother's Day would ever be satisfying. I dreaded my first Mother's Day as a parent without kids.

I have a friend who is a minister. For some reason, she thinks I can do things that I know I can't. The week before, she asked me to lead the congregation in prayer during the service on Mother's Day. I'd never led anyone in prayer before. I didn't want to. I'm not involved "that way" in church. I'd never talked to God out loud before. And why did she pick that day to have me try it? During the week, I agonized over it. It wasn't fair that she picked me, a noncustodial mother, to do it. It was just too hard.

I did it. I thought about motherhood in much broader terms than my own situation. I thought about mothers who have surrendered their children for adoption and mothers whose children have died. I thought about mothers in South Africa and Central America whose children are in jail. I thought about the Silver Cross mothers who lay a wreath each Remembrance Day. I thought about people who wish they were mothers and aren't. I thought about mothers who are far away from their children, mothers whose children are ill. My friend, who I thought didn't know me, knew me very well. Thinking about all those women on that particular day helped me a great deal.

New Year's Eve

Ron recalls his "first" New Year's Eve. At this time, he had been separated three months and was still enjoying access to his children. He was celebrating the new year by building a dressing table for his five-year-old daughter.

The children were with their mother, celebrating at a house party with family and friends. At 10:00 the phone rang. It was his little girl.

"She told me her brother was sleeping, but she couldn't because it was too noisy. She felt alone, she said. She wanted me to tell her one of my stories."

Ron is torn between happiness and longing as he relates this story nearly a year later.

"We talked for an hour and a half," he recalls. "It was a cute conversation. She finally fell asleep; the receiver just dropped to her chest. I didn't hang up because I didn't want her to get that noisy sound on the phone that alerts people their phone's off the hook. Someone came and got her at midnight and put her to bed."

Your child's birthday

One mother confessed that she was immobilized by her daughter's upcoming birthday. "I knew it was coming," she said, "and I knew I should be sending a big boxful of love through the mail. She lived a thousand miles from me. But I kept putting it off. Then I thought of phoning her. But I couldn't do it. It seemed so *wrong* not to be with her, I guess I pretended that the whole thing wasn't happening. I'm ashamed that I let that happen."

That mother was me. I had expected that my daughter would live with me; I thought it had been arranged. But a judge declared that she should be with her siblings and they had chosen to live with their father. I learned of the decision two weeks before her birthday and I let the day pass. Eventually, I did write to her and send her a gift, but I saddled myself forever with a mental video of a little girl waiting for the letter carrier to deliver her gift on her day. She was eight. I failed her.

Return to sender

Rose has a different story about a birthday gift. She had fled her marriage and put six provinces between her husband and herself. At her new secretarial job she kept mum about anything personal, unable to admit that she was a childless mother. For four months she worked among strangers who knew nothing about her except that she was quiet.

Rose said nothing about her three children or the letters she wrote them trying to express her love, trying to explain her absence. Every letter was unanswered. Rose said nothing about her daughter or that daughter's upcoming tenth birthday. She did not let on the agony she felt trying to find a suitable birthday card that did not read to *our* daughter or "You're another year older and we've watched you grow." She could not confide the pain she went through trying to find just the right gift for a little girl so far away.

On the birthday, Rose was depressed. She considered staying home and allowing herself the luxury of tears, but then became determined to go to work.

"I had to go and pick up the mail for the office. There was a parcel card there and I picked it up. I didn't know if I was going to faint or throw up or what. It was just so hard." Her birthday parcel had been returned with "refused" written across it in ugly black letters.

Rose returned to the office and a sympathetic boss extracted her story. Eventually the whole office learned of Rose's loss. She gained some supportive friends.

Hannah worked out a way to overcome some of the difficulties of a birthday in a separated family. She talked about feeling panic at the thought of her 11-year-old son's birthday. She wanted to be with him. She knew he wanted to be with his dad, too, and she couldn't face another "pretend" family celebration. Hannah also realized that he wanted to invite his friends to his house for a party. Eventually she moved the day of the celebration. A few days ahead of the actual day, she now invites him and one or two of his friends out for dinner and some fun. She is proud of the way she has handled this.

Know yourself

Graham learned a lesson from his first Christmas and subsequent special days. And he discovered a book that helped him prepare for his second Christmas: *Unplug the Christmas Machine*.[1] Although it wasn't written for separated people particularly, its suggestions can apply to everyone. Graham says the authors believe that Christmas can be happier, fuller, if people spend time thinking about their traditions.

"I spent a lot of time in the fall thinking about Christmas. It's a very important time for me, and I knew I was going to be alone. I had to sit back and say, 'What are the traditions? What is it about Christmas that I like and that is important to me and my own childhood? How can I re-create my own traditions?'

"My parents used to have an enormous party and invite everyone they knew. I decided that a big party like that was important, and since I didn't have any Christmas decorations, I made it a tree-decorating party. Everyone brought one decoration. And we sat here and strung popcorn and cranberries and I made eggnog with an old family recipe and put on a big spread accompanied by Christmas music. That was the first time I invited people in. It was also a sort of declaration that this was my place."

There could be nothing quite so disappointing to a child as seeing and smelling and touching a favorite cake only to bite into it and find it made of ashes. Better to be shown a second or third favorite dish that is real.

So it is with any cherished celebration for the child in all of us. Setting ourselves up with phony trappings can only leave us with the taste of ashes lingering in our mouths. No one wants to endure that every 12 months. The more we can learn about our own needs, the better.

Parents who have lived through a year without their children advised that special days should be planned carefully. Some rituals from the marriage will have lost their meaning and become hollow. Do some thinking alone and have some discussion with the children to find new expressions of the occasion. If you do, you may be in for some very pleasant surprises.

Recognize that different people need different things to help them feel good. Now is an opportune time to look inside yourself and find out what those needs are. Honestly.

Do your best to convey those needs to people who care about you. Going over to a friend's home for Christmas dinner might be what *they* need to feel good, but if they are truly concerned about you they will try to understand that it isn't necessarily what *you* need just then.

And finally, although you cannot erase the mental video of events past, you can add new scenes to it.

6

The Visits

Not having custody is always having to say goodbye.

Most of us grew up believing that children visit their parents after the children become adults. With the U.S. recording 1,150,000 divorces in 1996 and Canada recording 71,528 divorces the same year, tens, even hundreds of thousands of young children now visit their parents not by going down the hall or into the kitchen, but by getting in a car, on a bus, or into an airplane.

As divorce and separation change the structure of the family, these visits are becoming more normal. There are few classrooms in the country that do not have some children who live in single-parent households.

Most parents say that it takes time to get used to the business of visiting with their children and that many factors influence the tone of their visits. The ages and number of children are one consideration. The mental space of both children and the parent is another. Does the joy of seeing the kids override the grief of the separation, for example?

Other issues bearing on the visits are the setting in which they take place (a new location, a warm home, or a sparsely furnished apartment in a crowded area of the city) and the length of the visit. (Do we have two hurried hours or the whole summer to catch up and talk?)

If the children have just left a parent whose parting words were "Have a good time!" they will be happier and more relaxed than if the last picture they have is of the parent sobbing uncontrollably or shouting angrily, "Tell him I want that check today!"

Another influence is how long the child and noncustodial parent have been apart. If it's been a long time, both may be uneasy. Emotional distance between acquaintances and friends is to be expected after a long absence, but emotional distance between parents who have changed the diapers of the visitor seems unnatural. It takes time to melt the ice.

During the first few visits, both child and parent begin the job of establishing who they are to one another in this strange new set of circumstances, testing out their relationship with one another, exploring the limits of the old, and searching for the horizons of the new. The possibilities are endless. They are also frightening because they are unknown.

It's as if the beautiful sculpture that you've worked on for years has been destroyed by a tornado. Most of the pieces are there – somewhere – scattered around. But the pedestal it sat on is gone forever. You can attempt to glue it all back together the way it was and set it on a different pedestal, you can construct something else entirely, or you can use some pieces of the old and create new pieces to add different dimensions.

On one hand, you want things to appear as "normal" as possible. On the other hand, they aren't normal, so why pretend they are? When your child visits, do you throw the food on the table the way you do when you're alone? Or do you get out the silver tea service that belonged to your grandmother? It's up to you and the child to work that through.

The other major influence on the visits is the kind of non-custodial parent you are. Noncustodial parents could fall into five different categories.

1. Close, with a good relationship with the custodial parent.
2. Close, with a not-so-good relationship with the custodial parent.
3. Distant, with a good relationship with the custodial parent.
4. Distant, with a not-so-good relationship with the custodial parent.
5. No visits.

Living close to your child

The most fortunate noncustodial parents are those who live close to their children and who have a civil relationship with the other parent. These are the parents who have what is closest to joint custody. The children live with one parent, but frequently visit the other. They can often bike, bus, or walk to the other's home. They can stay overnight without it being a big hassle and can get to school without problems. They can phone the other parent for a quick good night or "How d'you do?" and know that the phone call will be private and accomplished without interception or recriminations. According to studies, and good common sense, these children and their parents are happiest.[1]

When geographic distance is not a problem, sometimes antagonism between the parents is. The children may have additional problems with split loyalty. They feel disloyal to Dad when they are at Mom's and disloyal to Mom when they are with Dad. This could mean that kids feel disloyal all the time.

When one or both parents overtly or covertly send out signals that the other parent is bad, cheap, a spendthrift, crazy, mean or whatever, the child feels frightened about visiting that other parent.

We do well to remember that our children are a mixture of both mother and father. Attacking the other parent is like attacking a part of the child.

As one wise man said, "If parents are out for the last pound of flesh, the kids are usually the ones to give it."

Although living close is better than living far apart, there are difficulties.

Not enough time

Graham, still fighting for joint custody of his four-year-old son and seven-year-old daughter, sees the children every Wednesday evening and every other weekend. He finds saying goodbye traumatic. So do the children.

"Sometimes my son says, 'I don't want to go back to Mommy's house. I want to stay with you.' So I'll sit down and talk about what the judge said. The last time, my son said, 'I think you ought to talk to that judge.'"

One of the things Graham finds particularly difficult is accepting the role of parenting that he threw out when he and his wife first decided to have children.

"I rejected the parenting role my father played – namely, absent parent, home on the weekends.

"My proposal is to see them [more] each week. Wednesday is a write-off. I pick them up at 4:00 or 4:30 and have to have them back at 7:30. That's barely time to come home, make them supper, and take them back.

"From my point of view, parenting happens in the routine. You can't sit down and say, 'Okay, now I'm going to parent you.' It happens at odd moments.

"If you see your children every Wednesday for three hours, you don't want to fight with them. The basic temptation is not to discipline them. And if you have them only three hours, why not just take them to McDonald's? Especially at the beginning, my insecurity was so high that I thought I needed to do something new and special for them every week. I didn't trust that just being with me would be enough. Now, after a year, I'm much more trusting of that.

"Now I can serve them a sandwich and soup for supper and they're perfectly happy. I don't have to buy them things, don't have to have a new and exciting place for them to go. They can be part of my routine and be perfectly happy.

"To me, the parenting happens in the stories that we read together at night. It happens when I insist that they brush their teeth, or when I cut their nails and they don't want their nails cut, or when I make them wash their hair when they don't want to."

Graham resents the artificiality of the time blocks his visiting rights inflict.

"I resent not being able to get them up in the morning, get them dressed, and drive them to school, even though that would be a great invasion of my life. I have a nice routine now. I have a nice long shower, a couple of cups of coffee, read my morning newspaper. It's wonderful. I love it.

"But my experience of those children has been that the most important questions they ask, they ask out of the blue. In the grocery store one day we were walking along down the cereal aisle and my son said, 'Why can't we see God?' So from my point of view, you have to spend time, you can't get around that."

Graham says that when he knows he'll have the children, he keeps his calendar clear – nothing and no one will interfere with that time. He is theirs. He also says that he's different when the children are with him.

"I change. Every time the kids come for the weekend I get terribly domestic. I get all this energy. I wash dishes, do the laundry, clean the house, bake – I've got six million things going on. And when I take the kids to the park, I'm not just parenting my kids, we get games going for the neighbor kids; I'm parenting 20. I love it."

Kids feel it, too

It isn't just parents who rage against the artificiality of the visits. Kids do, too. One father's apartment was a bus ride away from his two teenaged boys. He told them he would pick them up anytime. Both had bicycles.

In view of the boys' ages, no formal arrangement was ordered for visits, but the idea was that they would visit freely and whenever it was convenient for them and their father.

"From the time I left in October, to December, I saw the boys about once a week. I'd take them to the movies or a game, whatever they wanted to do. I tried to have them to my place to eat, or sometimes we'd eat out. My 16-year-old was quite angry. He told me he wanted to see me, but he didn't find it 'normal' to have to come across town to do it.

"And I didn't want to be a 'Sunday Daddy' either. I suggested that they bring their homework and come after school and spend the night as if it was a normal situation at home.

"The idea didn't work. The boys' mother didn't feel it would be good for their routine.

"That's what I wanted the most – it was always artificial to take them out to the movies on command."

The ending of this story is that three years after the split the father has remarried. His 16-year-old son has turned 19. He moved in with his father six months after starting university.

Living far away from your child

When the noncustodial parent lives at a distance from the child, time and money play a big part in how this situation works out. Visits are likely expensive and infrequent, and they may be difficult to arrange. If the relationship is good between the parents (or if court orders are followed), the expense is often shared. If the child is young and cannot travel alone, undesired contact between parents may take place, creating tension for everyone. Sometimes a mutual friend can act as go-between, picking up and dropping off the child.

When plane tickets are required for a visit, two things come into play: how often a trip can be taken, and the pressure one naturally feels when the visits are infrequent and expensive. The pressure could be summed up like this: "This better be worth it. We have to talk, talk, talk. We have to *do* things. We *must* have a good time together."

There is also the expense of long-distance phone calls to the children. Phone calls are more difficult, though, if the relationship between the parents is not-so-good. It can be extremely frustrating if the other parent answers the phone and wants to "sort out some stuff first." The temptation is not to call at all.

Children have never been known for their love of letter writing, so the mail is not a reliable method of communication. Sometimes the parent isn't sure that the mail is getting to the child.

One advantage of living far away from your child is that the visits are usually longer; that is, there is a bigger block of time and the visits have time to evolve into a more natural time together – everyday tasks are completed together, a routine can be established.

Staying with friends

Carole has moved from custodial parent to noncustodial with "no visits," to "close but not-so-good," to "distant and not-so-good," within her six years as a separated and divorced person. Her son is 11.

Carole has visiting rights two days each month. Sometimes she lumps the days together to get a weekend with her son.

Once or twice a month she boards a bus and travels four hours to another city. To help with her poor financial situation, she stays with friends.

"My friends are very gracious and kind," she says, "but it isn't home. I'm a guest in someone else's house. I can't do many of the things I'd like with my son. I'm always having to modify my plans. We still have a good time, but there are many things I ache to do with him that I can't. It's a different environment."

Between visits, she sends him cards and letters and phones as often as she is able.

One of the things Carole talked about was her son's friendships with kids she doesn't know. Friends are such an important part of children's lives (and increasingly so as they get older) and noncustodial parents such as Carole miss out on this important aspect. She would like to get to know some of them, but there are two obstacles. First, the time she has with her son is limited and she is jealous of sharing it with anyone. Second, because she is not in her own home, she is somewhat reluctant to invite her son's friends along, feeling that they would be an additional imposition on her host.

Out of sight, out of mind

Ann has lived at a distance from her four children since their father took them to live in another province. There has always been antagonism between her and her ex-husband.

She has seen her children during the summers and once a month for the past seven years. The court ordered that she and her husband share the cost of airfares. For the first five years the children flew to her. More and more lately, she flies to their city and stays with her mother to visit them.

Ann thinks that the four children, now in their early 20s and late teens, separate completely their "home" life and the time they spend with her. "There is no crossover," she says. "They don't talk about what is going on at home, and presumably the reverse is true."

Giving a gift to them, she says, has always been like putting it into a black hole. Ann never sees it again.

They don't phone one another very much. Ann doesn't phone because she doesn't want to talk to their father. She doesn't know why they don't phone her. "I'd feel much better if they did, but I guess it's just 'out of sight, out of mind' for them. The kids seem to keep their two lives separate."

Relationships don't stay static. Ann's son is now in university, away from home. Shortly after he moved, she received a phone call from him. "Can you come up [a five-hour drive] and go out for dinner with me?" he asked. Ann went.

Like many parents without kids, Ann has changed addresses a few times since the separation. Because she has lived in a "strange" place (compared to the kids who have stayed in the matrimonial home), her children haven't been able to "get into" the new place. Some children visiting a distant parent have never taken the opportunity to establish any sort of feeling of home. It's difficult for them. They don't know people. They may be in a totally unfamiliar environment – small-town people in a big city may feel out of place for a long time, and vice versa.

Helping the visitor feel at home

Unlike Carole and Ann, John remained in the matrimonial home after his wife left and the neighborhood stayed basically the same. Each summer when his daughter visited, she reconnected with her neighborhood friends. John and his new wife have worked hard to keep those friendships alive, both during the visits and in between. Both understand the value of this and they simply enjoy being with those kids. It's been another link through the years.

Over the 13 years that John has been a parent at a distance, he has seen his daughter alternate Christmases and every summer for six to eight weeks. They phone and write each other, but only sporadically. When she was very small, John used to fly to wherever she was living and pick her up and then take her back at summer's end. Since the age of 12, she's been flying alone. At Christmas, they meet halfway at his parents' house. He told me about how natural the visits were:

"I don't remember her being upset at all, talking about missing her mother or acting out. I don't remember her phoning her mother very much while she was here, but I imagine she did.

"It didn't seem to be a big deal, but perhaps subconsciously I've blocked out some of those memories. There must have been a period of adjustment when I remarried and then when the two children were born, but she got along very well with all of them.

"There's always a period of adjustment for me, of course. Like, 'Who's this little kid I have tagging along?' She'd have to adjust to a new set of rules and so on, but I don't remember any reticence on her part leaving her mother and coming with me. She was always very comfortable coming with me."

John's second wife says she thinks a big part of making the transition easier for the girl has been the fact that neither parent has ever played "games."

John's parents have also played a part in keeping the lines of communication open. "To my knowledge they haven't put down his ex-wife, and we haven't done it either. And I don't believe his ex-wife has put John down. Both have been faithful to that, not gone at the other via the child. In spite of everything, I don't think John and his daughter would be as close as they have been if that had happened."

Even though John and his family have now moved to another province, they keep in touch with his daughter's old friends. The first year his daughter visited their new home, they invited one of her old friends to visit at the same time. That way, the kids explored the "new territory" together.

When opportunity knocks, open the door

Parents at a distance usually plan for long visits. But once in a while they can take advantage of quick, unscheduled visits if the opportunity arises.

One of the more bizarre experiences I've had as a parent without kids occurred in an airport. It was May. I hadn't seen the children since the end of the Christmas break in January. One day I received a phone call from my daughter telling me that their father was taking them on a little holiday over the long weekend. They had 90 minutes at the airport where they had to change planes on their way home. Could I meet them there? I said I would.

I also asked her if she'd like the cat she'd left with me. He missed her.

I was excited and nervous. What would we talk about in 90 little minutes? What if the plane was late? What if I overslept and missed them?

I planned. I figured out my route by public transportation. I told the cat he'd love his new home. I decided on which small gifts to take, which recent photographs I had around to share with them.

Up early that morning, I tried to give the cat some rum and warm milk, hoping he'd fall asleep. He spit it out. I tried to stuff him into my knapsack. He clawed his way out. I tried to get on a bus. The bus driver wouldn't let me on with a cat. I paid more than $30 for a cab instead. I should have known then that this would be a bad day.

I found the proper procedures to send a cat airborne – buy it a ticket, buy a travel cage, and try to stuff the cat into it. I said a final farewell to the cat and left him yowling with the nice man.

I was at the appointed meeting place an hour ahead of time. The overhead monitor blinked that the plane was on time. I had a cup of coffee and went to the washroom three times. Each time, I made a mental note to "do something" with my hair. I looked terrible. Then I got nervous that they'd come while I was in the washroom, so I quit drinking coffee and concentrated on biting my nails instead.

The plane arrived, but the children didn't. There were a lot of children at the airport, most of them calling "Mommy." None of them meant me. The minutes dragged by. I could not believe it. Had their father said they couldn't meet me? Had there been an accident? Had they decided they didn't want to see me after all?

I went to the ticket counter to see if they were on the passenger list. They don't give out that information. I waited until well after the children's next flight was called. And then I left to cry. I don't know when I've ever felt so lonely.

When I arrived home, there was a message on my answering machine: "Hi, Mom. I'm so sorry. The tickets were mixed up. We come tomorrow, not today. See you then."

After spending all that nervous energy ahead of time, I didn't have much for the next day. I was simply glad to see them.

The children arrived, happy to see me and bursting with news of their holiday. We had chocolate milk and doughnuts and I showed them the photographs and some embroidery I was working on. It was a good visit.

The cat arrived at his destination, unscathed and sober.

No visits

Losing contact with the children is surely the worst situation for a parent. For one reason or another, the judge has decided that one parent will have no visiting rights. Very few cases are cut and dried. Not all cases are understandable.

The other way a parent loses the right to have visits is when one parent takes it away illegally, by kidnapping. Having children kidnapped from playgrounds is something many school principals and teachers have had to think about in the past few years. The hope lies in two areas: that children become adults, and that relationships and circumstances change.

Changing relationships

It is important to remember that none of the five groups noncustodial parents fall into is necessarily static. Some parents slip from one category to another. Circumstances change, arguments flare up, peace is made. One parent or both may move away.

In addition, as children grow up they will have more to say about how they want to spend their time. More and more, it will be *they* who decide on frequency, duration, and tone of the visits. Children will take what they need and give what they can – as most children do.

Growing apart

Gerald has moved from the "close and good," to "close and not-so-good," to "distant and good" categories throughout his noncustodial parenting (in five years).

Gerald lived close to his 11-year-old son for two years and then moved to another province because of an employment opportunity. He describes his attempt to maintain contact with his son:

"My wife got the house, so it was just natural that he stay on there. I tried to find an apartment that would be suitable and not too far away. My main concern was getting one where he'd be able to stay on weekends.

"The idea was that at least one weekend and maybe a couple of nights a week he'd stay with me. But that didn't work out because he had all of his things at the house and he'd get pretty bored at the apartment. I didn't have much furniture and only a little black and white television.

"At first, I would go over to the house to prepare his lunch. It was one of those horrendous things where I was making meals for him in what had been my home and no longer was. It was pretty difficult. Usually we'd end up going to a restaurant rather than do that. The second year he moved to another school closer to the apartment. Then he'd visit a little more often since it was 'on the way home.' That was better."

Gerald's other three children had grown up and left home by the time the marriage ended. He says the youngest one "rolled with the punches more than the others did" and believes it was because many of his friends were in the same situation.

In general, Gerald feels that his son's visits were marked by boredom.

"The feeling I got was that he was 'doing his duty, spending time with his father.' There was an artificiality to the visits. It was as if they were contrived.

"We'd try to do things together, but I was suddenly single, and he was suddenly an only child. The others were close in age and had left home the year before I left. He'd never been without at least one of them around before."

Most of the activities Gerald and his son discussed were far too expensive for Gerald's limited finances – skiing, go-cart racing, water parks.

Two years after the divorce, Gerald remarried. After Gerald and his new wife moved away, his son told him he wouldn't come for Christmas. Gerald was upset. He spoke a letter onto an audio tape and mailed it off. His son listened to his dad's voice, then commented to his sister that he "was missing his dad a lot." He decided to join his dad for Christmas.

Since moving away, Gerald tries to keep in touch by phone about twice a month and he is also fortunate with his work. Business trips take him back to his old province twice a year, so he manages to visit those times. His son comes out during the summer and sometimes at Christmas.

He misses all of his children, he says, but with the youngest it's a little different. The older ones would be on their own whether Gerald had left or not. He says there's more of a sense of responsibility with the youngest, and a sense of guilt.

Gerald and his wife now have three young children. His visits with his son have taken on a new twist. His son has gone from being the youngest of four children, to an only child, to the oldest of four when he visits his dad. It's balancing act. But so far, with love and luck, the visits continue and are "okay."

I asked Gerald if he harbors the hope that one day his son will live with him again.

"I've given up hope of that happening. I know things can change at any time, but his visits have been getting more difficult as he gets older. He hasn't made friends out here. Unless you go to school or get a job, how are you going to meet people, especially as a teenager?

"When he visited last summer, his phone bills were horrendous. He was phoning his friends a lot and managed to wipe out two months' allowance with no difficulty. He's very closely attached there.

"I think if he'd made friends here, or if there was something for him to do, it would be different.

"We invited one of his friends to come out for part of his visit. One year it worked, the next it didn't. It's hard with teenagers."

Reconnecting

The estrangement felt by Gerald began to disappear six months after our interview. With great excitement he informed me that his son had written to say he wants to live with him while he finishes his final two years of high school. Gerald, his wife and her children were busy preparing the welcome mat for this happy and unexpected turn of events.

Perhaps a more dramatic story is that of Rose. She left an abusive relationship under the worst conditions – she fled. She probably couldn't have had contact with her children even if she was living next door. The antagonism between Rose and her ex-husband has been frightening at times.

Rose wrote to her children for seven years. At first, the letters and parcels were returned and she knew she wasn't getting through. Then, suddenly, the letters were accepted. What she didn't know was that the letters and parcels were not given to her children. Her ex-husband collected them at the post office and hid them in the back of a closet. Her son was 17 when he discovered the cache.

Change came with a program on CBC television:

"One night I was watching a documentary film about children from broken homes. I was feeling so very far away from the kids and wondering how long it would be before I heard their voices. The program was over about 15 minutes when the phone rang. It was my brother saying my son was trying to get in touch with me. He gave me a number to call.

"I couldn't dial that phone fast enough," Rose said. "The next words I heard were, 'Hello, Mom?' He had been watching the same program. We talked and cried for 90 minutes.

"He said they had been lied to about why I left, that he had found the parcels and letters and cards behind some blankets in a closet and knew I'd been trying to contact them over the years. He'd also been in touch with some of his father's relatives. One thing the children noticed as they got older was that their relatives had kept photographs of me. It made them think that their mother couldn't be 'that bad' if even they kept pictures of her."

The call gave Rose the courage to make the long journey back to see the children. She was scared. By the time she went, it had been almost nine years since she'd seen her children. She took along two women friends for support.

Rose didn't tell the children she was coming, fearing her ex-husband would find out and sabotage the visit. She was clever in her planning, too. She made two visits: one to see them, and, knowing that they would be surprised and probably not know exactly what to say or ask, she went to visit friends for a few days and then returned to see the kids again.

"I was prepared for them to say, 'Get lost, why bother?' I knew they'd been lied to. I was scared, but I was prepared to answer any questions they had."

Like a detective, Rose found out ahead of time where the kids would be the day she arrived in town. It was summer. Two of them had summer jobs.

"My middle child, Shelly, was 15. She was working in a dress shop. She was all alone, and I walked in and she did a double take and then she said, 'Mom,' and we hugged and cried and then she phoned someone to relieve her and we went to the motel where she called her brother.

"He walked in the room, stood in the doorway, and looked at me. I started to cry right away and we walked toward each other and he put his arms around me and cried and cried and cried. My two friends went for the first of many walks so we could be alone.

"He didn't say much. In fact, I was a little disturbed. I thought, he's just like me, he holds it all in. But when I came back for the second visit a few days later we talked more."

Her youngest child, 13, had been four when Rose left. Their reunion, too, was full of tears and questions and reassurances. "She followed me around like a shadow," Rose said.

The children told her they'd hated her for a long time. "I said, 'Yes, I believe that. I hated myself, too.'"

Rose had taken along some of the things the children had made her long ago, treasured, handmade gifts. She also took the letters, parcels, and cards that had been returned to her.

"I didn't know if the opportunity would come up for me to give them to them, or if it would be the right thing to do. The outfits I'd bought didn't fit them anymore of course, but it was the right thing to do. They were glad I'd brought them along."

Although contact with the children has been sporadic at best since that summer two years ago, Rose still hopes that the children will establish more regular contact with her on their own. In the meantime, she continues to write them regularly. The son has left home to begin college, so interference from his father will not be a problem.

Changing expectations

Once we recognize that the visits feel artificial and awkward to both parents and children, once we accept that feeling as normal and as part of what all parents and children experience, we can begin to think about what we will do about it.

The danger in not recognizing the feeling, or in thinking that this is the way it will be forever, is that we miss an opportunity to change the visits, to be creative about them and get the fullest amount of pleasure from them.

Although it is quite natural to resent the constraints and artificiality of visits, we cannot leave it at that. We may end up giving the children the message that we resent *them* and this is the exact opposite of what we want to convey.

Finding out what's normal now

Some of us are more worried about what noncustodial parent-hood means than are the children. One father was looking forward to his 11-year-old son's visit after school one day soon after the separation. He cleared his calendar and left work early to be there when his son arrived. He thought carefully about what to serve him for dinner. He looked forward to being with his son; he missed him.

By 4:00 the father was home waiting, but there was no son in sight. At 4:30 the son phoned. "Hi, Dad! I'm over at Ted's to play for a while."

The father was hurt. But what did the son's actions show about how he felt? Not that he was callous or that he didn't love his dad. It showed that as far as he was concerned, he was in a normal situation, that he was relaxed, that nothing was "wrong."

Had he met his father at the door, anxious and trembling, or resentful and angry, or had he not called but simply gone off to play, there would be cause for alarm. The son has no concept of the father's sense of loss.

Another example of this is with my own teenagers. When they come to visit they sleep a lot. At first, I sat out in the living room, breakfast table set, ready to parent like anything to make up for lost time. I was determined that *we were going to have a nice time!*

I soon realized how silly I was. When we had lived together I let them sleep; why wouldn't I do that now? In my experience, unless teenagers are in love, sick, employed, worried or upset, they like to sleep in. For them, sleeping *was* having a nice time! I realized that they are tired, normal, growing teenagers. And I am grateful they feel relaxed and at home enough to sleep in.

Disciplining the visitor

Graham raised an important point when he said that the temptation is not to discipline the children on visits. Especially if the visits are short or infrequent, it may be easier and quieter to ignore the need for it. But it is dangerous to the relationship, to the child, and to the parent to allow rude remarks or other unacceptable behavior to become the pattern.

Graham wanted to have a nice time with his kids and not have it marred by tears or sulking or anger.

Another father, whose children (13 and 12) had decided to live with their mother, said that when the children acted up or fought he felt like saying, "Listen, you decided you don't want to live with me. Why come here, then, and make my life miserable? Go fight at your mother's."

In thinking it over after the children have gone, the parent may find the reasons for the behavior to be quite clear: the child is feeling disloyal; the child wonders how far, with these new arrangements, he or she can go; the child may be checking to see if the parent still cares enough to discipline (I often wish my children would just ask me!) – and so on. But these are usually thoughts we have in quiet moments, not at the time the child has just had a big fight with his or her sibling and kicked the dog.

Reminding yourself of what you always knew about discipline is helpful. Parents need to establish some form of discipline in order for the child to learn acceptable ways to live in the world and in order for the child to learn to discipline him or herself.

Children will be more secure knowing that even though the circumstances of your lives have changed, *you* are still the parent and still the same person you've always been.

Checking

Graham spent three weeks with his four-year-old son and seven-year-old daughter the first summer he was separated. Well aware of the turmoil in their little world, he kept checking and listening for obvious signs of distress that could lead to problems in the future.

He says that the visits during the first winter were predictable. The children would be glad to see him and suddenly his daughter would become very stubborn about some little thing and they would argue and she would cry. The issue would be blown out of proportion.

Eventually, she'd calm down and put her arms around him and they'd have a wonderful weekend.

"When I'd ask her about it, she'd say, 'I don't want to talk about it.'

"When we were together for three weeks, we had a few scenes. She'd be on my lap, crying away, and we weren't making any progress with what the crying was about. One time I said, 'Listen, I'm tired of this. You can cry all you want, but go somewhere else and cry.' She responded by saying there was nothing I could do about it.

"Then I suggested that maybe she was sad because Mommy and Daddy were separated. She immediately got defensive and said she didn't want to talk about that. I asked her when she felt this kind of sad and she said, 'When Mommy gets angry with me, then I feel scared.' Then she said she wasn't just sad about one thing."

Their conversation ended there, but Graham kept listening for more clues to help his daughter. Subsequently they had another talk during which Graham told his daughter that it always helped him if he talked about his feelings. Graham has recorded the conversation in his journal and reads it aloud during our interview.

"She said that it might help me to talk, it might even make me feel better if she talked, but it wouldn't make her feel any better.

"She then said she could sometimes talk to Barbara, a friend, and that helped, but not talking to me. I said I could understand that because it was sometimes more helpful to talk to friends than to talk to my mother or father. I then asked what she wanted me to do the next time she got into this situation. She said, 'Just hold me and not talk about it.' I told her that's what I would do. She asked if we could talk about this tomorrow and I said yes."

By allowing the child to be in control of her sad feelings, Graham apparently released his daughter to a deeper level of communication than they had had previously. Six months later, the crying stopped.

It is interesting to reflect on this father's response to what he at first thought were temper tantrums. What would have happened if he had picked her up and put her in a room to "have it out"? What might have happened if he'd shouted at her? How might she have responded if her father had not respected her grief?

The farewell

It didn't register with me at first what was happening when my eight-year-old picked a fight with her brother shortly before it was time for them to leave me. Nor did I understand when good manners and behavior deteriorated as the time grew near for another visit to end.

Finally, I understood what was going on: it's easier to leave when you're angry. Anger can be like an armor against our vulnerability. The anger can catch an unsuspecting parent off guard. "Forewarned is forearmed," Grandma used to say.

The teeter-totter

When one parent has sole custody of the children and the other has visiting rights and pays child support, a strange, uneasy teeter-totter game comes into effect. One worries about money and the other worries about not having his or her children's time and love. Each has something important that the other wants. Sometimes it becomes a sinister game: one sabotages visiting days; the other doesn't deliver the check and vice versa.

While it is true that sabotaging visits and witholding money are effective "weapons" to use against an ex-spouse, they inadvertently become a weapon against the children as well. Unless the child is in danger from the noncustodial parent, it is difficult to imagine why custodial parents make it hard for visits to take place.

After interviewing the parents for this book, I believe that one of the main reasons parents do give up their visiting rights or refrain from calling more often is that they cannot bear the hostility from the custodial parent, nor have they the energy to run the obstacles that custodial parents wittingly or unwittingly erect. They simply run out of energy for the battle and give up.

Recently, the courts have recognized that children lose out when their parents play these teeter-totter games. In some jurisdictions and in some circumstances it is unlawful to withhold child maintenance, and wages may be garnisheed if maintenance is held back. Although many will argue that there aren't enough "teeth" in this law and that parents still do renege on their payments, the law is being more rigorously enforced.

This move, however, tipped the uneasy teeter-totter in favor of the parent with the children. Throughout the interviews, I heard repeatedly that the parent with the children has the power. They felt that if the custodial parent feels negative about them or the visits, the noncustodial parent has little recourse.

The courts try to determine the "best interests of the child," yet this goal is a "gray area" that causes separating families great anguish and muddles the lawyers and courts. It is not difficult to distinguish between a loving parent and one who beats his or her child. It is easy to see that if a child doesn't have proper winter clothing, the child will freeze. These are simple and absolute extremes. The gray area comes in when one parent insists, for example, that the other drinks "too much" and is uncomfortable having a child around that lifestyle. What is too much? When the parent passes out? When he or she "gets silly"? When he or she has a glass of wine every night with dinner?

And values cloud the picture further. One parent may insist that the children go to church or temple each week, feeling that without certain religious teachings the children will be harmed. Will they? Will a judge rule on a question like that?

Parents' rights groups are saying that contact with their children is as important as money is for raising healthy, well-adjusted kids. Bitter custodial parents, struggling to pay the bills, may not agree with that. But it makes sense to me that a parent who is encouraged to visit his or her child regularly will take more of an interest in the child and the child's schooling and activities than one who rarely gets to exercise his or her parental duties and rights.

A number of provinces in Canada are passing or are in the process of considering a "Child Access Bill" that will make it unlawful for a parent to be deprived of the right of visiting with his or her child.

While a bill like this is good in that it recognizes the importance of the child's continuing relationship with both parents, there are two factors hindering its implementation.

One is that some parents feel that contact with the other is indeed bad for the children and should be stopped. They are

primarily speaking about cases where the parent has been physically or mentally or sexually abusive. Here, there is justifica-
tion. One of the problems with this, however, is that not all
allegations are true. According to a Montreal clinical child
psychologist, in the 1960s the best way to get custody was
to accuse the other parent of infidelity; in the 1970s it was
homosexuality. Now it's sexual abuse.[2]

When an allegation is first made, visiting is stopped or se-
verely limited and an investigation (which may take up to a
year) is launched. Damage is done not only to the accused
person's reputation, self-esteem, and bank account (in fighting
the accusation), but also to the parent-child relationship. As one
parent said, "You're dead meat, even if it's proved untrue."

The other factor hindering the implementation of rights to
child access, in my view, is that no one can legislate good will.
Or being kind. Or being nice. If the child does not want to be
with one parent because of what the child feels or hears, no
law can fix that problem. Only time and patience can repair
this particular broken bridge. An old Scottish proverb speaks
to us 260 years after it was recorded: "A pennyweight of love is
worth a pound of law."

A pilot project in Alberta, Canada, offers new hope to
divorcing families. In 1997, the government instituted a man-
datory parenting-after-divorce course in six communities. The
point of the course is to alert parents to problems they and
their children will face as they all struggle to reestablish their
lives, and to offer solutions. Parents with children under the
age of 16 who apply for legal separation or divorce, and who
live within 100 kilometers of one of the six communities, can
benefit from the course. (There are some exemptions allowed.)
A similar program is offered in Manitoba, but it is voluntary.

Visits are strange things to have with one's own children.
Particularly at the beginning of the separation, they require

forethought and emotional, as well as physical, energy. The last chapter in this book, "Letting Go, Getting On," includes some help in thinking them through and making plans for them.

7

Who Am I Now?

I remember my daughter coming over to my place shortly
after I'd left the marriage. I asked if she'd like to stay
for dinner. She responded, "I'll phone home and ask if I'm
allowed." Only a noncustodial parent can understand
how I felt hearing those words.
It was obvious I wasn't in charge anymore.
Was I like her grade two playmates? Or a visiting aunt?
Or a teacher? Just who was I, anyway?

When we first became parents, we knew that our children would not live with us forever. We knew they would grow up and move away. From the time we first change a diaper to the time we send them out into the world is generally less than 20 years. Almost all parents face the day when their children no longer live with them.

All parents also know that although we may refer to the children as "ours," we do not own them. As the years go by and children enter school, we soon realize that friends become as important to them as their family. By the time they reach their mid-teens, it is doubtful that families are as important to them as their friends. It seems teenagers are never home, except to sleep, eat, and change their underwear.

Even with this knowledge, we expected that our children would be with us as they grew. We expected to holler, "You're never home!" at them. We expected to *be* a mother or father. Noncustodial parents still are, sort of. But not in the way we thought we'd be and not in the way our kids expected us to be. For us, it's backward. The children have not left us. We have left them.

At first, noncustodial parents may see their situation solely in terms of loss and destruction. I heard myself using the word *ashes* when discussing this with interviewees. When I think of ashes, I think of the worst possible forest fire, probably dating back to my childhood, when I hid under the theater seat during the great fire in the *Bambi* film. But my next thought is always of the floral emblem of the Yukon Territory, the fireweed.

This beautiful mauve flower is the first new growth to spring up after a fire. I remember seeing miles of fireweed when I drove through an area where several thousand acres of forest had burned in the Northwest Territories. Remembering the obscene devastation and the hope springing from it never fails to remind me that nature is creative, strong, undefeated. We are part of nature. We can be like that, too.

Losing the old role

Regardless of whether we think about it consciously or whether it remains part of our unconscious, we carry a personal "job description" around in our heads. We are many things to many people. I am daughter, sister, writer, and so on. For 15 years, I was also mother. I wanted to be a mother when I was young. I trained for it with my dolls and my younger brother and sister. When my children were in school, I applied for a job as school secretary. I was asked the question, "How well do you cope with confusion?" I looked the interviewer straight in the eyes and said, "I'm a *mother*!" I got the job.

When I wasn't *doing* it anymore, I removed it from my resume. Initially, I didn't know if I was still a mother or not. Who was I now?

One father who believed in shared parenting says that he'd always regarded himself as part of a team. When his two children decided they were tired of the two-week on, two-week off joint custody arrangement and would rather live at their mother's full-time, he felt that he'd been "shoved off the team," relegated to "stick boy" or "bat boy."

"It's as if they've said, 'You can still watch us play, but we don't need you now.' I liked playing and I was a good team member. I don't know if I want to sit on the bench," he says.

I think this feeling of not being needed or wanted is common and is one of the reasons some noncustodial parents drift off into the sunset. Their money is still needed, but not their presence. And if the separation has been a bitter one, the feelings can be intensified by anger and sometimes hatred.

At cocktail parties or the hockey arena, you can hear the angry single parents: "S/he just doesn't care about the kids! S/he is never around!" For some parents without kids, the feeling of being unwanted overrides the desire to build new bridges. It's easier to give up.

Finding a new role

When I asked interviewees the "Who am I?" question, it was evident that their answer depended partly on what they think parents are and which parts of the "job" they had fulfilled. Some roles parents mentioned were caregiver, nurturer, friend, playmate, teacher, disciplinarian, launderer, housekeeper, nurse, provider, cook, chauffeur, role model, and coach.

Thinking about these roles can offer the noncustodial parent some new opportunities. For example, if a mother felt that she didn't have time to be a playmate when she lived with the child, she could now decide to fill that playmate role – to satisfy herself and her child.

If a father felt he would like to have done some cooking, but didn't because his wife was always so efficient in the kitchen, he may choose to experiment when the children come to visit.

Noncustodial parents cannot do all the things that a custodial parent can, but there is an opportunity to try some new things from a different perspective. There were certainly times in my life as a full-time parent when teeth brushing and homework reminders got in the way of conversation. I wanted to talk, discuss, explore. Now, those "maintenance" items have been removed. When I do see the children, we can talk. I have to assume that their teeth are clean when I'm not there.

It's important to spend some time "navel-gazing" about the "Who Am I?" question. Pretending to be someone we're not is hard on the nerves – of everyone. Pretending we are still part of the nuclear family, for example. Pretending that we still live with the children, pretending that we aren't sad, pretending that we aren't happy sometimes, too. Pretending that the kids are happier than they are; pretending that they are more upset than they are. Pretending that you're dating. Pretending that you aren't. Pretending that you've been victimized. Pretending that you haven't been. (We are all on both ends of this at one time or another.)

Finding our new role will take time and patience, and from the interviews, I learned that each person handles it differently. The main point these people made, though, is to be who you are. When we step back from the day-to-day responsibilities of childcare, what is left? Only loving them and showing it. Making sure they understand that you still care about them, are open to their joys as well as their sorrows.

It is important to be patient with ourselves, to love ourselves in this way, but it is difficult. It may be wise, as several interviewees said, to get some professional help. Professionals are available, trained, and willing to help. While it's true some are expensive, some are not. Psychiatrists, counselors, psychologists, ministers, priests, rabbis, mental health works, doctors, and nurses can help you. Joining a group of noncustodial parents may help (or starting one yourself). Reading about how others cope can help, too. Even when it feels that way, we are not alone.

Loving myself, too

Many of us have been taught to put others before ourselves, and we feel guilty – selfish – for thinking it should be any other way. This is a time to put those teachings on hold for a little while. Racing around trying to please others in an effort to regain some self-worth may not be what we need right now. Because you are still important to your children, you need to take care of yourself for them.

During the first six months of my separation, I was living in the mountains. It was beautiful there and I was fortunate to have such spectacular scenery around me as I faced the turmoil within.

I rented a large one-room suite from a divorcee who lived on the main floor of a wonderful 100-year-old house. I remember being grateful to her: she understood my alternating need to be alone and my need for company. She was someone I didn't know very well, but since she, too, had gone through separation and divorce and was a sensitive person, she knew exactly what I needed.

The suite had a fireplace in it. My matrimonial home had a fireplace, too, and when the family had been together or when we had company, we lit a fire. I would have never dreamed of lighting the fire when I was alone in the house. To me, wood was something you either worked hard to harvest, transport, split, stock and carry, or bought with hard-earned money.

I love a fire. It makes me feel warm inside and out. It fascinates me to watch the flames. It soothes and relaxes me.

Being in that quiet place in the mountains, knowing that someone was downstairs who cared about how I was doing, I began to think about what lighting the fire had meant. I thought, "My family was worthy of the fire, my friends were worthy of the fire, but I was not."

The empty fireplace and I lived together for more than two months. One day I lit it, just for me. I was loving myself.

I didn't light it every day after that, but I did light it on occasion. Each time, I thought about how lovely it was, how relaxing, how I was worthy of this special treat. It became a symbol of loving myself, giving myself a gift.

Who am I now?

When noncustodial parents were asked this question, many of them reflected on what the loss of role felt like in the beginning. The question, "What do you do?" is so much less personal and so much easier to answer. "Who are you now?" is tougher, and although most of the interviewees had moved beyond the initial pain, the question elicited emotion. The word used most often – or a variation of it – was wounded.

Graham, 13 months after separation

"Who are you, Graham?" I asked. He took a minute to answer. "Then, I was Graham – parent, teacher, 'together' person," he says.

"Now I am wounded. Now I'm a separated person, and for people who have been separated that speaks volumes. I'm a separated person with a continuously bleeding wound because I don't have my children; it's continuous pain.

"If it's been a very painful breakup, as mine has been, it's a loss of innocence. The world is not as perfect anymore. My friend refers to it as the Black Hole. You know what having your whole life come apart is about. And life will never seem quite so easy again.

"Not having custody of your children is a little like being an amputee. You're missing something; there's some part of you that's somewhere else. Anyone who wants to get to know you has to get to know these shadows that follow you around, because I don't come alone.

"People at work who didn't know me prior to the separation, who didn't know me when I was going home for lunch every day, who didn't know me when the kids were here almost every week, they didn't have that understanding of me as someone closely involved with his children. They only know me without attachments. Then they walk into my office and see all the children's artwork on the wall and they must think, 'What's this all about?'"

Hannah, four years after separation

Hannah's answer is unequivocal. "I'm a Mother." Four years after her separation, one child is married, one lives with her, and one lives with his father. Hannah has reconciled herself to the living arrangement now, partly because the children are old enough to come and go as they please. She realizes that if they had all stayed in one household, the children would be leaving or thinking about leaving because of their ages. What she thinks about now is what many mothers of adult or older teenage children think: What do I do with myself now that the children are grown?

Hannah is thinking beyond the mothering she has done and is thinking about enrolling in university soon.

Rose, ten years after separation

Rose still has a difficult time reconciling herself with the knowledge that the little kids she left are now almost grown. The missing nine years cannot be replaced. Rose still looks forward to making a meaningful connection with them, getting to know them personally again. But she is doing something about her inner turmoil since her visit with them. While continuing to write them and make herself as available as she can, Rose is beginning to tell her story. She is traveling now, speaking to groups of people in an effort to both alleviate her pain and to help others see that when a person cries for help, it is society's responsibility to try to help – and not judge situations by appearances.

In addition to this, Rose is working to understand what alcoholism does to families. Currently, there is a lot of interest in helping adult children of alcoholics and most bookstores carry books on the subject.

"I'm a wife, secretary, a mother trying to reach through the years to my kids. I'm a public speaker," she says. "And I'm healing."

Ann, seven years after separation

Ann answers the "Who am I?" question easily. She is a minister in a church and the mother of four children who live with their father. She says it took her about three years to accept the custody arrangement. Her ex-husband has remarried, and although that caused her some anxiety, she has accepted that. The woman is good to the children and "seems practical."

"It appears her relationship with the kids has been good," she says. "I told myself that the more people who show your kids love, the better it is for them."

Although Ann says that in retrospect she probably would have used some caution and had more legal advice about custody before separating, she seems to have adjusted to her noncustodial status well. She is cheerful and well-liked by her colleagues and congregation. She is a sympathetic and realistic adviser.

John, 13 years after separation

John took a long time to respond to the question. "Ever since I've been staying home with the kids," he says, "it's been a hard question. It depends on who I'm talking to, how I'm feeling." Then he straightened his shoulders and said, "I'm a domestic engineer, a house husband, that's about it."

I asked how he responded when asked how many children he has.

"Usually I just say two and then I correct myself and say three, because [my daughter] is basically part of our family, when she chooses to be."

Ron, one year after separation

"I am a father," Ron declared in answer to the "Who Am I?" question. And then he added, "A father who is being deprived of his children." Ron continues to define himself in terms of the work he does, but the overriding sense of victimization and loss of his rights and privileges seems to make him defensive. It's important to him that people understand exactly what happened, that he doesn't *want* to live apart from his children, that he was and is a good father.

Carole, five years after separation

"I'm a mother," Carole answers emphatically. "My whole life was in preparation for being a mother. All my other roles I relate to that primary role. People are the most valuable thing on earth, and the most valuable people are children."

Carole thinks that in our society parenting can be an isolating job. She hopes that single people and parents without their children will lend a hand in supporting parents and families. Carole, at a distance from her own children, enjoys being with young people and sees one role of society as helping to raise happy, healthy children.

Peter, one month after separation

"Since this happened, I've been on a roller coaster ride," he said. "My self-esteem has gone to hell and back again, but I'm stabilizing and I know I'm a worthy person. I do the best I can."

Peter thinks that because of what he's gone through he will be more effective in the classroom, more aware of what some of the children are going through. His long-term objective is to help those kids.

Crisis: new perspectives, different choices

We have a choice. Einstein is reported to have said that you cannot simultaneously prevent and prepare for nuclear war. In the same way, you cannot simultaneously rage against the past and plan for a hopeful future. We must choose. It doesn't come all at once, and it doesn't come when a specific number of days have passed. It comes when we are prepared to move forward in peace.

At one time, my job was to check to see if the teeth were cleaned, the socks in the laundry hamper, the homework done. That isn't my role anymore. My role is to support and love my children within the limitations of distance from them and the amount of money I can spend on stamps, long-distance phone calls, and airline tickets. My role is to remind them over and over again that they are loved in a very special way by someone who cannot see them every day. I do not want to be a "Disneyland Dad" (or Mom). I want them to know I care. I want them to remember always that I love and cherish them.

My role is to deal as well as I am able with this separation from them, to set some goals for myself, and to be an example of a decent human being. My role is to maintain my emotional, mental, spiritual, and physical health. It is to show my children that even when one of life's most earth-shattering events occurs, I am able to deal with it well. They, too, will face adversity in their lives. What example can I set them?

My role is to enjoy my children's visits, to be open to their questions and comments. My role is still, and forever will be, to love them. Who am I? I'm still a mom.

8

Letting Go, Getting On

If you are the kind of person who likes to fix things, people or relationships, you must get used to the idea that you cannot "fix" all the bad feelings separation and divorce create.

One of the wonderful things about humans is our ability and desire to solve problems, to make sense of our world. But when we first lose custody of our children, it seems to be too much to handle. We shrink within ourselves for a while, knowing instinctively that we must heal a little before moving forward. Friends may say, "You'll get over it." I don't believe we "get over it." But I *do* believe that we have the capacity and desire to move forward.

We make choices throughout our lives about everything, from which corner of the sandbox to sit in, to when we are ready to reach out to others in certain ways. Noncustodial parents have a choice to make about dwelling on the past or moving into the future. This chapter is written to remind you of things you may have learned in the previous chapters and to help you begin to let go of what can't or shouldn't be kept.

Being with your kids

The obvious thing that part-time parents do with their children is load them into the car or on a bus and take them somewhere – the zoo, the park, the game, the museum, the movies.

While these are good activities, they have drawbacks: they may be expensive; they may set up an expectation that you will provide entertainment; they may replace real communication with your kids when you and the children need it most.

There are hundreds of magazines and books that deal with how to raise children, how to deal with different ages and stages of development, how to do "fun" things with children. If you have not spent a great deal of time alone with your child and are feeling a little panicky about what you'll do during your time together, race to the nearest library and start reading. Even if you have been a main or participating parent, reading a book or two might be a good refresher for you.

My eight-year-old daughter loves to make things. When she is coming for a visit, I begin to save things for her – toilet paper rolls, nifty-sized boxes. I also check to make sure I have felt markers that haven't dried up, construction paper, and glue. Needles, thread, and fabric are always on hand. Making things is more than just an exercise that keeps her busy. This is family tradition for me and for her. When she was very small, we spent hours together making doll clothes, cards, gifts for people. It is one way we communicate.

Graham, too, finds making things with his children a happy form of communication. "What I really want to do is create memories for them," he says. "As an adult, I don't remember the day-to-day stuff about being a kid. I remember the special times, the rituals."

One day his daughter, seven, said she'd like to make some nut bread. Graham had no idea how to do that, but promised they'd do it during her next visit. He did his homework, found a recipe, bought the ingredients, and practiced the art.

"We did it," he said happily. "And then she invited all her friends in and gave them some. When it was time for her to go, she asked if she could take a piece back to Mommy. I'd already done some thinking about that and I suggested she take the whole loaf back and take a piece to school for her lunch."

I hope he took a photograph of his daughter standing on a chair mixing up the dough. Photographs are memories you can touch.

One woman I met was redecorating her new home. Her daughter had chosen the wallpaper, curtains, and other decor for her room. Even though the project took longer than it would have had they been living together, the sense of ownership that the girl had was healthy and she was rightfully proud of herself. A tendency among all parents to do things for the children is normal, but the rewards of participation can be great, especially in a split family.

Something that may be worth considering is a new hobby for the two of you. If you've always wanted to be a better photographer, perhaps now is the time to work on it – with your son or daughter. If the child is willing, can you afford a camera for him or her? If not, can you share the one you have, or rent or borrow one?

Reading up at the library on how to take good pictures can be something you can do together. Going for a walk in any kind of weather to take photos can be fun. Waiting together with breathless anticipation to see the finished photographs for an hour while you have lunch or a snack or until the next visit can be part of building your new relationship.

Other ongoing projects that you can work on each visit are worth considering, such as sewing a quilt, making a bird feeder or a doorstop, or working on a puzzle.

The benefits of this type of communication are many. Not only has the child (and perhaps you) learned or practiced a skill, not only have you "stitched" a memory, but the child will have something tangible that you worked on together, a reminder of the special time you shared. It is also easier to talk when the hands are busy. It is far less intimidating to children than having an adult sit them down and say, "Okay, now we're going to have a little talk."

Can you and your children agree on some form of activity that might benefit others? At Christmas there is always a need for people to serve dinners to people in need, or sort toys for disadvantaged children, for example. Or maybe you'd like to shovel a walk or do some gardening for an elderly person. The possibilities are endless and the benefits are many for you, your child, and whomever you help.

Games are another activity you can do together, even with young children. They need not be games where someone wins. (Actually, this can be a communication stopper.) There are noncompetitive games available, games where cooperation is the key to success, not beating your partner into the ground. Old standby games can be converted to be more cooperative, too. In our family, until the children are older, we don't keep score. The object of a game of Scrabble, for instance, is to see if we can use all the letters. You may be able to find games that encourage conversation, too, such as Scruples.

Communicating may not even take the form of conversation. I have vivid memories of sitting with my mother while we sewed, saying nothing, just "being," and of walking down to the barn with my dad, desperately trying to match his stride as *we* went off to work.

Sometimes parents make the mistake of trying to re-create the feel of a nuclear family without all the family members present. It doesn't work. You have to create a new family – or families. It is like trying to "retie the knot" in a piece of string that has been cut. The trouble is, the cut ends are always visible. We need a new ball of string.

While some family traditions are worth keeping, others belong only to the marriage or to that particular home. Use as much imagination and energy as possible to establish new ones. Unless the children are babies, they can take part in the planning of events and celebrations.

One mother told me that her weekend to visit landed on St. Patrick's Day. She isn't Irish, but she decided to celebrate anyway. Although her son thought that green mashed potatoes were a little odd, he soon joined her in the kitchen and was happily preparing a completely green dinner with his mom.

Maintaining contact between visits

Depending on your visiting rights and the geographic distance between you and your children, there may be days, weeks, or months between visits. Reestablishing contact is easier if there hasn't been a complete break between visits. Maintain as much contact as possible to let the child know he or she is loved and is important to you.

The phone is one obvious method of keeping in touch. The success of phone calls depends on many things: how old the child is, whether you can afford long-distance charges, whether your ex-spouse is willing to pass the phone over to the child, how comfortable the child feels talking to you while the other parent is in the room, how comfortable you feel speaking to your ex-partner.

There are so many "ifs" in the situation. Here are some hints on phone calls that I have gleaned from reading, from interviews, and from experience.

1. Teach your child how to make collect calls. Suggest a day and time when you're most likely to be home.
2. If you find the calls frustrating because you ask the questions and receive a one-word answer, search your mind for common ground – weather, news, an update on the dog or cat, a project you started when last together. Try to phrase

your question so that a one-word answer isn't an option. ("What do you think about...?")

3. Try to find out when it's a bad time to call. Calling at supper time will annoy your ex-spouse. Calling during the child's favorite television show won't work, either.

4. Setting up a specific time and day to call the children takes away the element of surprise, but makes sense. But once a schedule is established, don't fail to call.

5. Don't expect too much, especially at first. Children must learn the art of conversation. A quick, reassuring "hello" and "goodbye" is better than long, awkward pauses.

6. Pay particular attention when your child mentions school and special friends (write down their names if you might forget) so that you can ask about them later.

The other obvious link with the child is the mail, and everyone loves to get mail – E-mail, snail mail, or fax. You needn't live at a great distance to send mail.

I have tried to write the children every Monday. Whatever I did on the weekend is fresh in my mind, and whenever it's Monday I know I have something important to do. If you don't think the children receive your mail at home, you may want to see if the school or a friend will accept letters for them.

Look for special postcards or cards that you think the child would like, especially cards for holidays or special celebrations, such as Halloween. You may want to include something small with the letter – a package of stickers, a cool bookmark, a magazine clipping or a cartoon, a photo from your last visit. Include self-addressed, stamped envelopes periodically. If your child has a pet, write to it in care of your child. Check out the world according to Fido. It's fun to do.

Don't be discouraged if your child doesn't write back. Some people are procrastinators, others hate writing letters. Kids are people, too.

Establishing a new relationship

If you are the kind of person who likes to fix things, people or relationships, you might as well get used to the idea that you cannot "fix" all the bad feelings separation and divorce create. What you *can* do is look after yourself, communicate your never-ending love and concern to your children, and be as open to them as possible.

Your feelings of resentment, bitterness, and rage should not touch your children. Do your best to make your home one the children feel comfortable in and look forward to visiting. If you can create an atmosphere of trust, your children can be open with you; they still need you.

I found it hard to tell my children how much I missed them. I was afraid, I suppose, of making the teenagers feel guilty about their understandable desire to live where they had friends, where they had grown up. And I was afraid my eight-year-old would feel disloyal if I mentioned it too often. After all, it wasn't *her* fault we were in this situation.

I did tell them I missed them. But I tried to balance it with telling them about happier feelings I had, and about how glad I was that they'd visited or written or phoned.

About a year after the separation, my teenaged son taught me a lesson with his silence. We were discussing school and I was playing the part of inquisitor: "*What* mark did you get in Social?" was probably how I reacted to his report that a test hadn't gone well for him.

Eventually I found myself nattering about the same old stuff I'd nagged him about when we had lived together. He didn't say anything. His silence made me consider my own words – and the fact that he'd made an effort to visit me.

I had to face the reality that my authority over him was almost nonexistent. First, because he didn't have to answer to me directly; he would soon be hundreds of miles away from me. Second, he wasn't a baby; he was a young man. Surely I could do better than *this!*

On his next visit, I tried to see him as he really is: an almost-man, a bright and beautiful young person with a lovely sense of humor, a boy who missed his mother even if she did nag, a young man very close to me who was visiting my new home. We had a lot of fun together.

Spending time with other people's kids

One of the assignments I had as a newspaper reporter was to interview the high school music teacher. As we talked, I was surprised at how many extra hours that man put in with the kids. He had bands for all ages and devoted many weekends and hours after school to teaching. When I dug a little deeper into his story, he explained in a gentle way that he knew that some of those kids had a hard row to hoe in life, that he was glad to give his time to them. He said he had kids, too, although they didn't live with him, and that he hoped that someone, somewhere was giving them something extra. I wasn't very professional. I cried.

The first Christmas I didn't have my children with me I felt lost. For 15 years, every November, I would haul out the box of pine cones, glue, scissors, dough and so on and the children and I would make small gifts and tree decorations for friends and relatives. Closer to the day we'd make an elaborate (we thought) gingerbread house. We made gift tags and gift wrap. We made cards. For two months the house was a relatively happy mess with sparkly things embedded in the carpet and glue where it shouldn't be.

When the first "separated November" arrived, I went out and found a friend who had a couple of kids and sat at the table with them and made wreaths. I just couldn't stand not doing anything, and doing it alone would have been too sad.

There are always "extra" kids around, kids who would love to do things with *somebody*. You could be that somebody.

Being realistic about your energy and needs

While it would be silly to rush out and join several groups or teams to fill the void, it is equally silly to quit activities which have given you pleasure and a feeling of self-worth. Balance and honesty with yourself are important.

John feels his involvement in the community helped him maintain his balance.

"It was important for me to feel involved, to feel there was something I needed to attend to, even if it could never take the place of the family unit or my daughter," he says.

Moving, changing jobs, death, and divorce place tremendous stress on people. You may be experiencing more than one of these forms of stress in addition to losing custody. Take stock of your situation realistically. While continuing some activities may give you a sense of continuity, it may also sap too much energy. While starting new activities may offer new growth and new friends, you may not be able to give much energy to the group and thereby set yourself up for disappointment. Staying home and reading a good book may be what you need to recover; on the other hand, you may be cutting out an opportunity for some much-needed positive strokes. Only *you* can monitor how you feel when the lights are out and you're alone. Only you can decide.

Your physical surroundings

Whether we have moved or not, noncustodial parents have an opportunity during the first changing weeks to reassess their physical surroundings – even including furniture and dishes. If they give you a neutral or happy feeling, then they should likely stay with you. But if they cause discomfort, bad memories, or seem just plain ugly – can they be replaced?

John said it was months, even years, before he could walk past his daughter's bedroom without a catch in his throat. His present wife describes it this way:

"The first time I went to John's house was two years after his wife had left, 18 months after his daughter had gone. One of the first things you saw in the house was a picture of his daughter, a beautiful eight-by-ten. You couldn't miss it.

"You couldn't really talk to John without knowing about his little girl. She was so close to the surface with him. She was always right there.

"Whenever you came through the front door, hers was the first room you saw. Sometimes he wouldn't make it past that before he'd be in tears, reliving that time."

She followed her instincts about what to do to help her husband. "One of the first things I did when we were together was redecorate that room and refinish the furniture. I don't know if I'd have done that anyway or whether I was trying to erase that for him."

While it may be that the child would like to return to his or her room on visits, you may think about redecorating it with the child. Or closing the door for a while.

Getting extra help

There are no extra points awarded for self-pity or guilt. If you can't cope with these feelings yourself, find someone to help you. If each day looks cloudy and rotten, do not walk, run to the nearest mental health clinic, church, synagogue, temple, psychologist, trained professional.

One man saw a psychiatrist for a few months. This non-custodial parent's advice is to get all the help you can, but make sure it's professional help.

"Friends are good and supportive," he said, "but they can't help you solve the problems. Go for counseling or therapy for as long as it takes you. Take it on. Do it and get over it. It doesn't take as much courage to do that as it does to grit your teeth for the rest of your life. We have to say, enough is enough, let's put these feelings behind us."

Keeping a journal

A few of the interviewees kept journals. For some, this was an entirely new venture. A journal can serve at least three functions. It is a record for any future legal action that may take place. Second, it is a repository for all those feelings that are racing through your heart and mind; it is a safe place to vent anger, fear, loneliness, as well as joy. Third, a journal can also be a record for your children. Obviously, we cannot explain to a two-year-old how we feel, nor would we want to. But some day, that two-year-old will be 22 and 32. Maybe an occasion will arise when he or she asks you just what happened, what was going on during that time. Perhaps then you will pour a cup of coffee, dust off the book, turn its yellowed pages and read aloud. A journal can build bridges into the future.

Changing the system

Carole has used her experience to try to help other people who lose or give up custody. She has become a "family law reform activist." She started a group in a city that had no previous support for noncustodial parents. She is fighting a long, hard battle to try to make the court system more fair to children and less confrontational for the parents. She believes that a tremendous amount of anger is generated within the system we now have.

As well as writing articles and briefs to politicians, she speaks to support groups and individuals grappling with this crisis. Telling her story, she says, is focusing the hurt, using that energy. "Sharing my hurt with newcomers to the scene helps to make some sense of it all," she says.

Relief

At first, feelings are strong, the wound deep. At times it seems the flow of emotional blood will never be stanched. One father who believes that "divorce is like death" draws the analogy of being at the deathbed of someone you love. The person is terminally ill. You do not want him or her to die. But when death finally does come, along with the sense of loss and intense pain comes a feeling of relief.

If the marriage had been a good one, it wouldn't have ended. Even those who did not want it to end will eventually agree that living with one who does not love or respect them makes a mockery of the relationship.

And for someone who has been involved in a bitter or sad or angry relationship, the silence one hears on waking in the morning can be a beautiful thing. It's true we miss our children fighting for their share of time in the bathroom every morning, but we do not miss living in a tense relationship.

While we were wondering what would happen, what the judge's decision would be, we were desperately trying to hold on. When the loss comes, and we rise each day to breakfast in the thundering silence, we know we need hold on no longer in that way. We can unclench our teeth, our hands. We are free to begin our grieving and our rebuilding.

The first few months are not only a time of fast changes, but of reflection and re-creation. We are at the end of something important. We are also on the threshold of new beginnings.

Notes

1
Point of Departure

[1] D. Hurley, ed., *Separation, Divorce and Remarriage: Psychological, Social and Legal Perspectives* (London, Ontario: Kings College, 1987), 37.

[2] Bruce Fisher, *Rebuilding: When Your Relationship Ends* (San Luis Obispo, California: Impact Publishers, 1981), 1-2.

[3] Phyllis Chesler, *Mothers on Trial: The Battle for Children and Custody* (New York: McGraw-Hill Book Company, 1986), 331.

[4] Bill Adler, *Motherhood: A Celebration* (New York: Carroll and Graf Publishers, 1987), 33.

[5] Chesler, *Mothers on Trial*, 383.

3
Guilt, Anger, and other Demons

[1] C. W. Smith, *Will They Love Me When I Leave? A Weekend Father's Struggle to Stay Close to His Kids* (New York: G. P. Putnam's, 1987), 109.

[2] Richard A. Gardner, *The Parents' Book About Divorce* (New York: Bantam Books, 1979), 52-53.

[3] Smith, *Will They Love?*, 223.

[4] Brenda Rabkin, *Loving and Leaving: Why Women Are Walking Out on Marriage* (Toronto: McClelland and Stewart, 1985), 214.

4
Other People

[1] Don Peacock, *Listen to Their Tears: How Canadian Divorce Law Abuses Our Children* (Vancouver: Douglas and McIntyre, 1982), 82.

[2] Ann Landers syndicated column, Saskatoon *Star Phoenix*, October 13, 1988.

5
Waking Up without the Kids on Special Days

[1] Joe Robinson and Jean Coppock Staeheli, *Unplug the Christmas Machine* (New York: Quill-William Morrow, 1982).

6
The Visits

[1] Hurley, *Separation, Divorce, and Remarriage*, 37.

[2] Grace Wong, "A Bitter New Issue," *Maclean's* magazine, October 3, 1988.